LOW HANGING TRUTH

RICK ENLOE

Low Hanging Truth

Illustrations by Rick Enloe

Cover Design: Matt LaCombe

First Printing: 2024

Printed in the United States of America

ISBN: 979-8-9892607-1-3

eBook ISBN: 979-8-9892607-0-6

Dedicated to The Marvelous One.

CHAPTERS: ACT ONE

1. Uncommon Grounds
2. Lunch Special
3. Tamper Proof
4. Gauze Burrito
5. Nuts on Fire
6. Senescence
7. Student Body Prez
8. Wonder Woman
9. How Am I Driving?
10. Never Trust A Trickster

CHAPTERS: ACT TWO

11. Tin Man
12. Travel Phobia
13. Neighbor Guy
14. Crumb and Queen
15. Big Guy Grocer
16. On A Roll
17. Javascope™
18. All Choked Up
19. On a Stick
20. Don't Know

CHAPTERS: ACT THREE

21. Better This Way

22. Imagine That

23. Don't Be a Dickie

24. All Night Shoe Shine

25. Going Backward Fast

26. Party Planner

27. What You Do

28. Sincerely Wrong

29. Biscuit Blast

30. Looking Down

31. Advice for Those I Love

FOREWORD

by Debbie Macomber

You are in for a rare treat. If you already know Rick Enloe, it will be no surprise. If this is the first time you've heard his name, be ready to be awed and entertained. Rick is a speaker, humorist, entertainer, writer, and storyteller extraordinaire.

For example, when I first met Rick, he said he was an Ancient Middle East history teacher. That was his clever way of telling me he was a Pastor. Let me tell you that Rick is much more than a man of God. He's a modern-day sage and mentor to many. Please don't take my word for it; you will discover his wisdom, charm, wit, and warmth through the pages of this book. Rick's stories are engaging and meaningful. I promise you will laugh at some and wipe a stray tear at others.

Several years ago, our team at Debbie Macomber Inc. launched Welcome Home Magazine. My goal was to share my world with my readers. This included books I read, the authors I love, recipes, travel tips, and gardening. Rick's column Low Hanging Truth became a popular segment my readers looked forward to reading. As a masterful storyteller, Rick weaved timeless truth into each issue. My readers and I were blessed by his contributions to the magazine.

Now, you will have the opportunity to experience his wisdom, humor, kindness, and understanding of human nature. May you come away filled with encouragement and strength, your heart warmed, your mood lifted, and your spirit lightened. I'm so delighted to share this dear friend with you.

Debbie Macomber

INTRODUCTION

Greetings

Welcome to LOW HANGING TRUTH! My name is Rick Enloe.

Right away, I imagine some of you must be thinking, "Yeah, right! How do I know Rick Enloe isn't an AI Avatar posing as an author? Chat GPT probably generated these 'short stories for the long haul' in 30 seconds as a part of a conspiracy to end books from real authors." I get it. But, while all of that is possible, I am an actual person, and I wrote this collection just like Moses wrote the Ten Commandments, tediously carving out each idea word by word, except I cranked this out on a MacBook Pro and we all know Moses used the Microsoft tablet.

I'm not comparing what I wrote with scripture, but I'm pretty sure somebody will use this book to start their own religion. It has a tree on the cover, and the title is a rip-off of low-hanging fruit, so...tree..fruit...I can see where this is headed. I don't recommend that, but if it happens, send ten percent of all offerings to Low Hanging Headquarters, and I will use it to feed hungry children. Five of them. Their names are Pax, Kai, Blu, Scotland, and Goldie. In the original Greek, all of their names mean "brilliant and hilarious." I will mainly feed them pancakes.

Moving on, many of us have heard the classic metaphor "low-hanging fruit." We get it. Things that are easy and within reach. It's that slow lob in the strike zone that we can crush. Here, it's the same big idea related to truth. The thing that makes this kind of low-hanging life lesson accessible is that it's wrapped in personal experience. The lofty truth, often abstract and remote, lives in libraries, but the low-hanging truth lives in our personal histories. Memories fade, but histories shape us. Each of us has stories to tell, shedding light on our discoveries. I hope that a few of these narratives resonate with yours.

Still, "truth" is a tricky word. For instance, what's the first thing you think of when somebody says, "To be honest with you..." or "To tell you the truth..."? When I hear these phrases, I think, "Is truthfulness just starting now? Have all previous claims in our conversation been fabricated?" We want to believe that being truthful is our default setting, but we know it's not. Why not? Well, sometimes the truth hurts. There is also the idea that we might hold conflicting truths from others, so we often settle for half-truths to avoid conflict.

For all these reasons, our quest is ongoing because we are not satisfied with "a" truth; we relentlessly search for the whole truth. The naked, unvarnished truth. Most of us are conditioned to think finding absolute truth requires a journey beyond our familiar surroundings to the highest peaks in search of a truth-telling sage. There is a common notion that truth is above and beyond us, in the exclusive grasp of the highly trained savants who have podcasts.

But what if the most reliable source of truth is also the most available? As in low-hanging truth. We are not looking at a mountain peak but looking within and seeing truth embedded in our realities; right where we live, in the events of everyday life, are daily gems of truth waiting to be mined, polished, and displayed.

A 'heuristic maxim,' commonly known as a rule of thumb, is credited to a Franciscan friar and philosopher named William of Ockham. His rule, Occam's Razor, suggests that "the simplest answer is most often correct." It is referred to as his frugality principle. The literal interpretation of finding truth is that explanations should not be multiplied needlessly. My interpretation? "Simple low-hanging truths, personal and common, are profound."

Truth has been one of the central subjects of oral and written history. When we hear someone expound on truth, we also wonder what makes their claim accurate. There are books and centuries of thought related to the nature of truth and how to find and verify it. Some of the "big-stick" thinkers of all time, back to Socrates, have spitballed answers and theories on truth.

One of my favorite authors is Belfast-born and Oxford-trained C.S. Lewis. He penned over 30 books that orbit around truth topics. He writes, "If you look for truth, you may find comfort in the end; if you look for comfort, you will not get either comfort or truth, only soft soap and wishful thinking to begin, and in the end, despair." Lewis sees comfort in truth-seeking but no truth in comfort-seeking. He tries to steer his readers away from living a life of "soft soap and wishful thinking," leading to desperation.

Have you ever been accused of wishful thinking? Assigning a false reality to a longing or constructing an imaginary fact out of a fragile desire is easy. Life is hard. When hurt takes hope's place, desperation takes reality hostage. Lottery tickets are sold on wishful thinking.

The opposite of desperate wishful thinking is inspired willful thinking. It's not what happens to us that brings us to what is true; it's how we evaluate and interpret our experiences.

Wishful people think, but willful people think again. They sit with their thoughts until they think it through.

Why doesn't everybody think willfully? Undoubtedly, it takes a serious investment of time, solitude, and silence. Willful thinkers are good at staring out a window and into space for hours. Gordon MacKenzie, author of Orbiting the Giant Hairball, illustrates this thinking when he comments on the miracle of a cow making milk. He observes how the miraculous bovine process consists mainly of the cow eating grass all day. This may seem like an enormous waste of time to the casual observer. The money is in the milk, so why not collect it more than once daily? That's not how it works with cows; somehow, this truth contradicts our hurried and harried lives. There's something extraordinary happening in the willful waiting.

This short collection of essays is primarily personal, with a couple of my favorite third-person stories. My intent is to inspire your willful thinking, leading to insightful conversations animated by your own low-hanging truth. Enjoy.

ACT ONE

Chapter One

1

UNCOMMON GROUNDS

"Maybe if we re-invent whatever our
lives give us we find poems."
— Naomi Shihab Nye

I am dedicated, as a Pastor, to the "parish model" of ministry. That means serving everyone in our community, both the "faith folks" who gather on Sundays and those who don't know what they're missing. My first invitation to serve as Pastor was from a church in the University District Parish in Seattle, Washington. Early on my first morning as Pastor there, I decided to take a lap around the immediate neighborhood and get familiar with some of the people and businesses adjacent to the red brick church building on the corner of 65th and Roosevelt. I pulled up my scarf and kept my head down as I rounded the corner on a brisk December morning. Looking up, I saw a colorful "GRAND OPENING" sign on the front door of the new restaurant called Uncommon Grounds. The cafe was the only storefront on the street without

Christmas decorations. At the top of the door was a handmade sign offering Turkish coffee and Middle Eastern pastries. At the bottom of the short menu was a bold "FREE PALESTINE NOW!" sticker.

I was interested for a couple of reasons. First, I love a good conversation around a cup of strong coffee. Secondly, as a teacher specializing in Middle Eastern history, I enjoy meeting anyone with connections to that part of the world. I pushed open the door, stepped up to the counter, and ordered a coffee.

"I am happy to have discovered your restaurant." I announced, "I look forward to being a regular customer."

"That would be so very good," replied Ahmed, the owner, joyously, "We have just opened for business, and during this cold weather, we have not seen many customers."

"I will tell others about your place," I said, turning and waving before making my way up the street.

I decided right then to stop into Ahmed's cafe every morning before heading to the church office. By the end of the first week, Ahmed would start preparing my drink when he saw me approaching the front door each morning.

"You have become my first regular customer!" Ahmed said with a smile, reaching for a handshake I firmly returned.

By the second week, I stopped taking my coffee to go and found a place at the counter where I could chat with Ahmed. He told me about his family in the Middle East and their passion to see a free Palestinian state. He shared his distrust of how Western media and churches portrayed his people. I listened and learned, never mentioning that I was the Pastor of the church around the corner.

Ahmed told me he hoped to support his family abroad with the profits from his cafe, but things weren't going well early on. "We don't have so many customers like you," he admitted sadly.

And that's when I put my 'Christmas cards' on the table.

"You know Ahmed," I said, "I am the Pastor of that church

on the corner, and I don't have that many friends like you either." I could tell it threw him back a little, but I hoped being a 'regular customer' would keep our new friendship alive. Ahmed slowly smiled and lifted his coffee cup. I smiled and raised my cup in return. It seemed like more than a coincidence that we were building a friendship at Uncommon Grounds on uncommon grounds.

Just a week before Christmas, while enjoying coffee at the cafe, I opened my Bible App and re-read the story of Jesus and the local fishermen in his hometown. These small business owners were struggling, like Ahmed, having worked all night to catch fish, yet they had nothing to show for it. I looked around, watching Ahmed take an order and then run into the kitchen to prepare it. I thought about Ahmed's journey and the hard work he'd invested in opening this cafe to help provide for his family. The Bible story reminded me that when Jesus provided a miracle for the fishermen with the record-breaking catch, it was the most significant day they'd ever had in the fishing business.

I began to wonder. What if our church could be a part of giving Ahmed his best day in the restaurant business and, in doing so, share the holiday spirit of love and grace with someone who needs to be encouraged and reminded that what he cared about mattered to us?

With Christmas only a weekend away, the Salvation Army bells were ringing on the corner, and I was teaching the final Sunday night class of the year at the church. I told the class of 50 people about Ahmed and Uncommon Grounds. I asked them if they would be willing to turn their class time into a field trip to the Middle East, complete with great coffee and falafels. I explained the idea of giving Ahmed his best day in business, just as Jesus had given his fishermen friends. I encouraged them to show the spirit of Christmas with generous gratuities. They couldn't have been more excited about trading a lecture for this holiday adventure.

I dialed Ahmed on speakerphone from the classroom and told him he had friends interested in coming over.

"I will get a table ready for you," Ahmed promised.

"Well, there's over 50 of us, so maybe you should get all the tables ready," I explained, holding the phone up for the class to hear with a big grin. Ahmed was speechless. I assured him it was true and turned the phone toward the class, who cheered wildly.

In less than five minutes, we descended on Uncommon Grounds. It looked like the opening night of a Hollywood premiere. The cafe seated 25 people, and everyone in the class 'party' agreed to wait in line until their table was ready. We created quite a scene. People driving past noticed a restaurant that was so good people were willing to wait in line for a seat. The holiday cheer was contagious. Many who stood in line had never talked to each other outside of class and began to forge friendships as they waited for a table.

Meanwhile, inside the cafe, Ahmed was laughing and clapping his hands, overwhelmed with gratitude for the outpouring of customers. I joined the cafe staff and jumped into service, seating people and bussing tables. Ahmed ran to the grocery store down the street every half hour for more supplies. Several hours later, as the last new customer left the cafe, I helped Ahmed put the chairs on the tables, swept the floor, and bid goodnight to my tired but happy friend.

The following day was Christmas Eve. I went down 65th Street and ducked into Uncommon Grounds for my morning coffee. Ahmed raced out from behind the counter and kissed me on both cheeks. Tears welled up in his eyes as he said, "Your friends have given me a night of great success. They have shown me what Christmas means!"

My eyes started leaking a little, too.

I discovered some low-hanging truth on the corner of 65th

and Roosevelt Ave. I learned how important it is never to let ideology kill hospitality.

Even though Ahmed and I started with uncommon histories, we built a friendship on the common ground of providing for our families. He had never celebrated the arrival of Jesus at Christmas, and I had never observed Ramadan. Still, we both had parents and children, and we both wanted to be a meaningful part of the community we lived in.

We can all forget the Parish principle, becoming isolated and irrelevant, throwing parties for those like us instead of thinking about how to add value to others unlike us. In doing so, we begin to live shallow and uneventful lives, missing out on the beauty and wonder around us.

Robert Waldinger, a psychiatrist and professor at Harvard Medical School, directed one of the world's most extended health and well-being studies by tracking the same group of 724 men for 80 years. In his now-famous TED Talk, Waldinger said, "Our study has shown that the people who fared the best were the people who leaned into relationships, with family, with friends, with community."

Those who lived diminished lives were the most isolated and insulated. This remarkable research reinforces another low-hanging truth: we gain and grow as we give. For some reason, we think that someone different from us who cares deeply for something we care nothing about or perhaps admires what we disdain is disqualified from consideration or caring. We can easily forget that our parish is everyone in our community, not everyone in our commonality.

So, who lives in your parish yet on the edge of your commonality? Go exploring. Introduce yourself. Sit in their chair. Listen to their hopes. Bus their tables and introduce them to your friends. Discover why Uncommon Grounds is the best place to build something new.

Chapter Two

LUNCH SPECIAL

"Nobody made a greater mistake than he who did nothing
because he could do only a little."
- Edmund Burke

What started as a casual early lunch at Bell's Diner quickly became a late-morning medical emergency.

The clatter of plates filled with the daily lunch special arrived at our table. At the same time, a woman screamed, and dishes crashed to the ground behind me. I turned to see the frantic woman standing up and desperately crying, "Help! Is there a doctor here?" A muffled thud followed her question. Her husband fell off his chair and onto the diner's floor.

I stood up and looked around to see if any doctors or medical personnel were reacting to the woman's call for help. As I scanned the room, I realized nobody was moving in response to her cry for assistance. I also noticed that I was the only one in the room without white hair, if they had any hair at all.

It helps to know that Bell's Diner is renowned for the best senior citizen lunch in town. For a low fixed price, Bell's offered a daily lunch combo: a cup of soup, half a sandwich, a piece of pie, and all the coffee you could drink. The Daily Special was enormously popular with the senior dining crowd, who generally arrived two time zones to the east for lunch.

The woman's cry for a doctor was accurately interpreted by all who could hear her (which might not be too many) for someone trained to intervene with the emergency technique called C.P.R., which stands for Cardiopulmonary Resuscitation. This life-saving intervention has been around since the mid-1700s. French doctors were the first to formalize the practice, mainly applied to near-drowning rescues. The guidelines for performing CPR have changed over the years, as has the diverse range of cardiac resuscitation events beyond near drowning to any event where someone's breathing or heartbeat has stopped. Initially considered a "mouth-to-mouth" technique, the rescuer administers rescue breaths; CPR has now been updated and augmented by the "chest compression" approach- where the first responder applies 100 to 120 uninterrupted chest pumps per minute. This happened during the rescue breath era. Right? Since nobody else was moving toward the distressed victim, I seemed elected to the position by default.

Up to this point in my life, I had never performed CPR, nor had I been trained to do so, but fortunately, I watched a ton of television growing up. I had witnessed CPR being administrated on television over the years. Who knew that re-runs of Baywatch (featuring David Hasselhoff and Pamela Anderson) would inadvertently prepare me for this restaurant rescue?

Channeling my inner Hasselhoff, I dodged the diner patrons, pushing chairs out of the way, and rolled the unconscious man onto his back, asking the hysterical lady what his name was. She pulled her hands away from her face and said, "Willard!"

I said, "Willard?"

She added, "Most people call him Will, but I've always called him Willy."

While informative, I could see that clarifying what I would call him wasn't contributing to his future.

I put my hands on his face, slapped them together, and said, "Willard... Will...Willy?" There was no verbal response; his eyes were half closed, and I noticed his lips turning blue.

The unfortunate reality was that today's lunch special featured the meatloaf sandwich. The rescue attempt would have been much less complex had Willy collapsed on ham and cheese day. To clear the airway, I reached into his mouth and pulled out a large bite of meatloaf, slathered in ketchup, and out came his entire upper and lower dentures. This dramatic development cleared his airway and emptied half the restaurant.

After preparing Willard for the rescue, I yelled, "Someone call 911!" I'm sure most people thought I said that on Willard's behalf, but I was also thinking I might need transport to a post-traumatic stress specialist as well.

I began CPR as I remembered it from the Boca Raton Beach rescue team. I was exceedingly less photogenic wearing business casual, kneeling on the floor of an inner city diner than on the beaches of south Florida where inspired young men in the prime of their lives would run toward the rescue in slow motion sporting the vintage red speedo.

I continued my version of CPR for ten minutes until the paramedics arrived and took over. To this day, I consider it one of the longest ten minutes of my life. I used the standard Baywatch technique of thirty chest compressions and two rescue breaths. For ten minutes! Had this been an actual

Baywatch rescue, the procedure would have been augmented by a couple of three-minute commercial breaks, causing the rescue to seem abbreviated. Not so in real life. Ten minutes is long, especially when the patient is not responding.

After six hundred seconds of effort, three paramedics stormed into the diner, administrated intravenous medications, then immediately loaded Willard onto a wheeled stretcher and sped out of the parking lot, sirens blaring, on their way to the Northwest Hospital trauma center.

I wasn't hungry anymore. I wandered out to the parking lot and stared out the front window of my car for a long time. After a half hour of deep breathing, I drove to the hospital, walked into the Emergency Room, and asked, "How's the guy from Bell's Diner doing?"

Having heard my question, the paramedic who transported Will exited the ER entry door.

"He's gonna' make it. Some guy gave him CPR until we could get there and saved his life."

I breathed a sigh of relief, and then it took me a second to realize, "Hey, I'm that guy!"

Later that night, as I laid my head on the pillow, I replayed the drama again and thought about what life had taught me that eventful day. I had performed life-saving mouth-to-mouth resuscitation. I began to think about what I had learned through this ordeal. Three low-hanging truths came to mind:

First, in a situation that calls for action, "don't get involved" seems like a default response, putting our safety first. I learned to pay attention to the secondary voice of empathy to overrule the passive first response based on the preservation of self. There are many things we cannot do, but why not offer what we can?

Secondly, even when not officially qualified, I can be helpful. Never underestimate the effect of doing something over doing nothing. How many of us would have children if we waited until "qualified" for parenthood? Most of what we do for good has been trial and error. We generally only step forward when we step up.

Lastly, I recommend that anyone suffering a medical emergency requiring a mouth-to-mouth response take a mint before collapsing. Your rescuer will appreciate it.

Chapter Three

3

TAMPER PROOF

"Life has a particular flavor for those
who have fought and risked all that the
sheltered and protected can never experience."
- John Stuart Mill

S o there I was Monday morning, bright and early, contemplating the fact that I had been using the same stick of deodorant for a whopping three months. Santa had put that personal hygiene savior in my Christmas stocking, and now it was the first day of spring. Talk about long-lasting freshness!

For 14 weeks, I faithfully swiped that stick under my arms, relying on its bold claims of a fragrant shower-fresh experience. It promised to "glide on clear" and be "body heat activated." I followed the simple instructions: "Apply to underarms only." I thought I was good to go unless a rash or irritation decided to crash the party.

I slathered away, day after day. No rash, but something peculiar was going on.

Body odor has plagued humanity since, well, forever. The underarm area, in particular, has been ground zero for some seriously spicy aromas. We've all experienced those dreaded wet orbs under our arms, a.k.a. excess perspiration or "hyper-hidrosis," as the fancy doctors call it. And where there's a damp ring, there's an undeniable reek, my friend.

Ancient Egyptians had a solution: shave underarm hair and apply scented oils. The Vikings took it up a notch to attract ladies from different lands (plus, the chilly Scandinavian climate helped suppress the underarm bacteria party). People have concocted hundreds of home remedies throughout history, but commercial solutions only popped up a hundred years ago.

In the late 1800s, companies began offering oils and rubs to cover the sweaty masses. Still, it wasn't until the end of the century that antiperspirant technology came along, aiming to stop underarms from sweating altogether (bye-bye bacteria, hello freshness!).

Then, in 1903, EverDry hit the market. It was so acidic that it ate through clothing and caused trouble. But the 1950s brought us rock and roll, hula hoops, and aerosol deodorants for underarm funk. These spray-on wonders contained aluminum zirconium and chlorofluorocarbon propellants, effectively battling the stink but also harming the ozone layer. So, while burning holes in the sky, one could only wonder what they were doing under your arms. Not worth it, right? Thus, they were banned in 1977.

Enter the late 1970s when the deodorant stick claimed its throne as the ultimate underarm odor warrior. It remains at the top to this day. Natural stick deodorants have gained popularity over chemical sticks because they're safe and eco-friendly. They're essentially mineral salts, just like the ancient Egyptians used. They may not be the most powerful, but I'm a stick user through and through.

Now, after three months of faithful use, I noticed something strange. My deodorant stick looked brand new, as if it had been resurrected from the pits of freshness. It never changed shape or color, standing tall on the bathroom counter, mocking the dying and curling toothpaste tube. I had stumbled upon the holy grail of everlasting perspiration relief!

But here's the kicker: the effect seemed more "pro-perspirant" than "anti-perspirant." That chalky white mini-monolith had zero deodorizing powers on my natural ambiance. It simply wasn't working. I applied it confidently, but the active ingredients were not in play.

The mystery unraveled early one morning when, upon close inspection under intense lighting, I found a nearly invisible plastic film protecting the top of the deodorant stick. It's known as a tamper guard. The odiferous process reversed after peeling the tamper guard off and contacting the target area. Now, an effective shower fresh deodorizer was at work at the expense of its former everlasting feature.

Morning after morning, I swiped away at my underarms, blocked from engaging the active ingredients.

The contents of the stick were protected but not productive. I had continued to believe a fragrant promise in the face of no olfactory evidence.

I had unwittingly found a non-aerosol personal hygiene parable.

What if I was just like this deodorant stick? Going through the motions without making contact.

Trying to protect myself from getting used by others. Isolating to preserve emotional inventory?

It seems reasonable to leave our tamper-proof seals on, keeping our distance from others, hoping we don't get used by the people we contact. It probably is reasonable and justified by experience, but it stinks to live like that. If we think about people we admire, it's not because they kept their distance and maintained their status quo. It's because they were willing to give themselves away, changing the world at their own expense.

People like Mother Teresa in Calcutta, India, or Nelson Mandela in South Africa were both "in the pits" of poverty and injustice, living without a tamper guard, engaging difficulty by contacting the most vulnerable in their unique situations. Keeping the tamper guard in place leads to living as a hermit, separated from others, holding, and hoarding to avoid losing what we have. It seems like our natural response to difficulty and hurt, but it is a stinking way to live.

Not many of us are working with those dying on the streets or leading a revolution against systemic racism, but we still face the choice to make something better at our own expense or to stay away for fear of the cost.

Say somebody we know experiences a profound loss. The urge to send them a note and quote something motivational tends to push back the instinct to reach out more personally. Life is crazy enough. Why not keep a safe, tamper-proof distance? An app on my phone can send a sympathy postcard, letting them know I care enough to coordinate my thumbs in a typing motion for 30 seconds.

It turns out to be very efficient and perfectly ineffective.

There is no replacement for time spent together, hugs, conversations, and freshly baked cookies. Reaching out and taking the tamper-proof shield off can also mean there will be tears and subsequent costs.

The late Nel Nodding, a Stanford professor best known as an educator who taught the ethics of care, talks about the difference between caring "about" someone and caring "for" them. We could care about many issues that affect people while leaving tamper-proof protection in place. This kind of care expresses itself as a concern. "I'm concerned about poverty and racism," which begs the more profound question, "Am I caring for anyone experiencing poverty or racism?" Nodding's ethic of care teaches that when we are willing to strip off our tamper protection and make actual contact with others who need friendship and help, we might get depleted, but in the process, we upgrade the fragrance of our world.

When considering caring at the cosmic level, the Bible employs the Greek word Kenosis to describe how Jesus cared. Kenosis means "to empty." In the New Testament letter of Philippians, the Apostle Paul encouragingly writes in his letter of encouragement to the people in Northeastern Greece.

"Think of yourselves the way Christ Jesus thought of himself. He had equal status with God but didn't think so much of himself that he had to cling to the advantages of that status no matter what. Not at all. When the time came, he set aside the privileges of deity, took on the status of an enslaved person, and became human! Having become human, he stayed human. It was an incredibly humbling process."

That part about setting aside the privileges of deity is kenosis. Privilege was the tamper protection that he removed. He had every right to maintain distance but emptied his rights by giving them away to those who had none. That's the mind-blowing part of his story. It's kenosis when somebody drops their guard, demonstrating inclusion and respect for those most excluded and disrespected. A religious bias informed the entire social system in this era against the poor and abandoned ones (still sounds kinda' familiar). The excluded ones smelled up the place. Kenosis will tear off entitlement and bring the fresh air of love.

So why not be "kenoso-tatstic" and tear off our tamper guards, set aside our privileges, and begin to make significant contact with others? We risk getting all used up, but we will not be wasted.

Thanks, Shower Fresh!

Chapter Four

4

GUAZE BURRITO

"Reality is easy. It's a deception that's the hard work."
- Lauryn Hill

T he early morning winds of November sent a chill through my nine-year-old body as I made my way to Horace Mann Elementary School in Rapid City, South Dakota. Home of the Hornets. At this time of year, the cold wind was as biting as the mascot. Even so, the icy wind was only a precursor to the dreaded upcoming real winter, with snow drifting to the house's eaves and ice forming inside the windows, creating the annual six-month struggle to stay warm at night.

Our house was somehow insulated for a southern climate, not the piercing Dakota winters. Even in the daytime, the single burner oil stove in the living room could never generate enough heat to change the temperatures in my bedroom at the opposite end of the house. The numbing cold was compounded at night when my Dad turned the thermostat from the red zone to the blue zone to save money on heating fuel.

Also, it wasn't just MY bedroom; my brother and I shared the room and slept side by side in a double bed between two oversized bedside tables. In the winter, the bed was adorned with a pile of covers to keep us alive, but no matter how many covers we used, the mattress felt like a cement floor. Each night, I could feel it pulling all of the heat out of my body while, at the same time, my brother was pulling all the covers to his side of the bed in an apparent involuntary response to hypothermia.

On a frosty Monday morning, I made the three-block walk to school, lowered my head, and pushed against the icy breeze, filled with frigid weather anxiety and winter dread.

I didn't know it at the time, but things were about to change.

"Good morning, everyone," our exuberant teacher started, "I want to share an excellent opportunity with you all."

I pushed the frame of my oversized black glasses to the bridge of my nose and leaned in, trying to see the colorful brochure she was holding up in front of the class.

"Anyone who wants to sell holiday greeting cards can help support our school with much-needed supplies while winning fantastic prizes! If interested, talk to me at our first recess this morning."

I could hardly wait until our first break when my intrigue turned to joyful anticipation as she unfolded the greeting card collection and showed us the list of prizes. "Of course," she beamed, "The more cards you sell, the bigger the prize!"

There were trinkets and puzzles for selling a box or two, but at the high end of the sales brochure, there were sporting goods prizes like baseball mitts or cool electronic prizes, including watches and calculators. But it was the camping gear that got my attention. Pictured next to the tent collection was a bright green sleeping bag.

A warm tingle ran down my neck when I saw that sleeping bag with its red flannel interior. I imagined zipping it up on a cold December night, sleeping like a baby through a Midwestern blizzard. With this sleeping bag, I would be insulated from my icy mattress, and as a bonus, my brother might pull the covers off of me, but he would not be able to alter my comfort level once inside this cozy, life-saving sleeping bag.

I headed home that breezy afternoon, realizing the only thing standing between my future survival was selling 36 five-dollar boxes of assorted holiday greeting cards. How difficult could that be?

My first sales pitch was to my mom, who would have appreciated a conversation about my new career aspirations before taking on the $180 obligation. After hearing me out and sensing my excitement, she commissioned me with a cookie and a kiss and said, "You'd better get to selling."

It took me three whole weeks, two hours each day, going door to door through our adjacent neighborhoods to sell all my cards. Each night, I would count the cash and store it in a plastic sandwich bag. Finally, I had the entire one hundred and eighty dollars. I'd never seen so much money in one place. My Ziploc runneth over.

I can't remember my feet touching the ground the following Monday morning when I brought the cash to school and proudly handed it over to my teacher. Along with the money, I had filled out a prize sheet with my name and address carefully, including a big checkmark in the premium prize division box and a circle around the green sleeping bag.

I would hurry home for two weeks to see if my prize had arrived. Eventually, my mom grew tired of being the bearer of bad news and said, "Look, if the box wasn't sitting on the kitchen table, never mind asking."

Then, after two weeks of anticipation, I made it home from school on a gusty December weekday to find a box on the table containing a return label from the Holiday Card Prize Department. I was stunned. It was the size of a shoebox. Did the prize department get my reward mixed up with someone else? Had my lush green sleeping bag with the red flannel interior gone to someone else's house, and I got their deluxe, but not premium reward?

Then, I opened the box and saw the sleeping bag. It was the smallest sleeping bag I'd ever seen. The green polyester exterior covered the thin red flannel interior. It looked like a World War Two bandage. I had imagined a suitcase-sized REI sub-zero-sized sleeping bag, and what I got looked like a gauze burrito.

And that's the day I learned for the first time what the expectation gap is.

The expectation gap is the street name for disappointment when what happens falls woefully short of what you were hoping for. We've all experienced it repeatedly in relationships, opportunities, and life's adventures.

It's the difference between the bright, colorful picture on the restaurant menu and the previously frozen and subsequently deep-fried meal that gets delivered to your table. It's the glowing and cheerful wedding day versus the ensuing marriage. The business partnership that falls apart when profits don't materialize. It's that gut punch when you are at the wrong end of the over-promised and under-delivered reality.

It's working hard and finding out you got worked.

It's getting the gauze burrito bait and switch.

So what do you do? You realize that there is still a low-hanging truth in the expectation gap.

You live and learn.

Once you know what it feels like, you never make anyone else feel that way.

You learn to keep a safe distance from "over-promise and under-deliver" sales pitches.

You stop exaggerating.

You realize why child labor laws are essential.

The Christmas card scheme was the first of many disappointing offers, but it gave me most of what I needed to know and grow from. The gauze burrito is my rally cry!

Chapter Five

5

NUTS ON FIRE

"Sometimes you feel like a nut, sometimes you don't."
- Leon Carr

O ur house has a garage, originally designed and intended to shelter motor vehicles. Still, it now serves primarily as a storage center for large plastic boxes stacked, labeled, and filled with home decor. The boxes are all packed with furnishings corresponding to the seasons and holidays we cherish and celebrate throughout the year.

Some seasons have multiple times more boxes than others. Christmas, the storage leader, is a collection of dozens of translucent poly containers. The contents vary depending on whether a given year has a red and green theme, optional elf ornaments, or a silver metallic look with reindeer influences. There are several boxes of Yuletide dishes and platters, and festive pillows are a constant in every seasonal collection. There are couch and chair, bench, bed, and deck pillows. Wall plaques and mantle items take up another couple of boxes.

The Christmas boxes are closely related to the Valentine boxes since some red touches can carry over. Then there's the two-box Easter collection, filled with wicker baskets, plastic eggs, and bunnies to celebrate the resurrection of Jesus, the great redeemer and provider of shiny fake straws and candy.

The "Patriotic" box is filled with Independence Day and summer furnishings. It has miniature American flags, stars and stripes cups with saucers, and a plaque that says, "Freedom is not Free." The flag for the porch and lemonade dispenser comes out of the Patriotic box but stays in service all summer.

The rotation of the boxes from garage to house and back provides tangible mileposts as the calendar year unfolds. It always seems bittersweet when the autumn box comes out of storage and into the day-to-day decor, signaling the end of summer. Beach toys and sea shells are swapped out for pressed burnt umber and russet leaves, sheaves of barley tied in bundles, and bags of assorted nuts. Nothing welcomes fall more than a handsome display of nuts. Walnuts. Pecans. Filberts. All dried and poured into a vase the size of a large goldfish bowl. A tall orange candle is embedded in the middle of the bowl of nuts, making the perfect harvest-time centerpiece for the table. This annual bowl of nuts surrounding an orange candle provided one of our home's most memorable autumn emergencies.

Autumn had gathered us back inside, around the kitchen table after summer's departure, and vacated the Adirondack chairs on the back deck. This shoulder season showcases sunsets in the late afternoon and invites the return of the Northwest wind and rain. Our house was adorned in complete fall seasonal decor, the contents of the autumn plastic box on full display while the box itself sat in the garage, empty as the tomb on Easter morning. We gathered our family of four around the crosscut oak dining table, lit the orange candle in the seasonal bowl of nuts centerpiece, said prayers of thanks, and shared comfort food around stories of our daily adventures. After dinner, the table was cleared, dishes washed and restocked in the cupboard, the children disappeared to finish homework, and I sat in my favorite reading chair to make progress on a Dorothy Sayers mystery.

The first thing that caught my attention was a hushed popping sound, almost a light tapping rhythm, coming from an adjacent room. As I looked up from my book, I saw smoke trailing through the top of the doorway to the dining room, and the smell reached my nose. I dropped the book, ran into the kitchen, and saw the centerpiece inferno. Nuts on fire! The candle had burned down and ignited the dried nuts in the glass bowl, and flames were jumping out of the bowl toward the ceiling. I immediately threw open the door to the back deck and grabbed the glass container, which was now too hot to hold on to, so I threw it out the back door. The glass container hit the deck and broke into pieces, and a hundred flaming nuts began to roll across the wooden deck. I ran outside and began kicking the fiery nuts one by one off the deck and onto the grass lawn below. There was just enough room under the deck railing to pass a nut, as long as it was kicked without altitude. I continued to kick the smoldering nuts, one by one, through the lower passage like a mid-fielder on a Valhalla soccer team. I scored a hundred goals in under a minute, avoiding the potential loss of our home by flaming nuts.

After airing out the house, sweeping up the broken glass, and picking up charred nuts from the lawn by the porch light, we made a cup of tea and realized how close we had come to catastrophic loss by centerpiece.

This experience allowed me to ponder some low-hanging truths about the damaging potential of things that become centerpieces in our lives.

Can the things we choose to decorate our lives with become destructive?

I know a guy who owned a primary home, two vacation homes, a yacht, several smaller boats, and vehicles for hauling, travel, commuting, and racing. Nearly all his waking hours were spent maintaining, servicing, or repairing what he owned. I've once heard him say, "I'm nuts to own all this stuff." Yep. Nuts on fire.

O.K. That seems like an extreme example of over-accumulation, but this is not just an issue for the privileged. Most of us have "burned the candle at both ends," trying to be everything to everyone, only to find ourselves burning out. Same thing. Nuts on fire.

Thankfully, when we are willing to acknowledge that our candle is getting destructively short, we can snuff the flame before a meltdown. Those closest to us can often sound the alarm, acting as our loving fire extinguishers. Together, we hope to shine brightly without flaming out.

Chapter Six

6

SENESCENCE

"You know you're getting old when you get that one candle
on the cake. It's like, 'See if you can blow this out."
- Jerry Seinfeld

S enescence is the biological term for aging. It's all the
rage. Everybody's doing it. I should be warming to the
idea of being called "Sir" by people with neck tattoos,
but I'm still surprised. I mean, I am in significant decay, and
there are people in various stages of fossilization all around me.
Despite all evidence to the contrary, I don't seem to believe that
I will get "really" old. And even if I do come to grips with my
fermentation, I conceive a different kind of aging. I envision a
more heroic and classier march to the grave. I anticipate major
capstone events, like lifetime achievement awards and invita-
tions to perform sagely TED Talks. Why don't I take my decline
seriously? I feel the aching joints and have impressive ear hair!
I'm probably only a couple of clicks from adult "nappie"
chaffing, but here I go, motoring on without reference to the
odometer.

It's a classic case of terminal contradiction. I can feel the sun setting, but I struggle to take the condition of my deterioration seriously. One thing that enables my "degeneration denial" is its sneaky pace. Aging is a creeping, deceptive, and inconsistent process that stays camouflaged long after it has arrived. If I focused my attention on the mirror daily, I would see incremental changes so subtle that I refuse to face the reality of... my...face. It's not that I am ultimately convinced of my immortality, but what I call delayed gentrification. That voice in my head says, "I know I'm bound to wear out..eventually...but not today!"

Then it happens.

I sprain my ankle while sleeping.

I flinch when startled by eye floaters, little specks of white darting through my peripheral vision like drunken moths circling the porch light.

Next, everything starts to slow down, including my attention span. I don't want to give up on my dreams, so I stay in bed longer, but even after getting up late, in a few hours, I am captured by the dawning awareness that a nap isn't going to take itself.

Then the memory starts to go. I saved the file but can't remember which hard drive to search. I started using the "Geezer Hack" for remembering passwords by changing them all to "incorrect," that way, I can enter any combination of keystrokes as a password, and the computer will respond with, "Your password is incorrect." Eventually, I'll forget even that move. Geezer Fail.

Another tell-tale sign of closing in on life's expiration date is the emergence of haphazard hygiene. For instance, after a shower, you think you have entirely toweled off, so you start to get dressed and find an entire section of undried acreage. Usually, culprits are the small of the back or under something, but occasionally, it can be a whole appendage, like the entire circumference of your left leg. This behavior flows from being easily distracted, having zero short-term awareness, and possible localized loss of hydro-sensitivity.

After years of successfully applying shave cream to my face and carefully maneuvering the four-bladed razor to rid my chin of unwanted stubble, finishing with a rinse, to discover that my face is only randomly shaved, I slap on twice the recommended amount of noxious aftershave cologne and head out for the day only to learn three hours later, I left a triangular strip of unshaven beard on the side of my chin, leaving the appearance of an attempt to grow the Picasso version of a goatee.

Physically devolving, I now consider walking an exercise. Where I used to do "sets" of weights and "circuits" at CrossFit, now I do "steps" encouraged by the congratulatory rings on my watch. As a result of my non-aerobic workouts, the sun may be setting in my future, but the height of my beltline is rising. Trading aerobic activity for walking is the slippery slope to CBD gummies and dinner at 4:30 in the afternoon.

After walking instead of running comes falling instead of standing. Aging tends to tamper with my balance, resulting in an eventual crashing sound. Long before the tripping ensues, there are the skidding and scraping sounds from my shoes as I lose the ability to keep my foot off the ground for an entire step. Once one foot catches the ground with a skid, the other foot careens ahead to cover for the lazy step. This works until the recovery foot catches a toe, and the fall is on. Falling is the fun part; landing is not so much. Younger people exercise options when landing to soften the plunge, like rotating mid-descent and rolling out like a rogue secret agent, diffusing the impact and minimizing the damage. The senior community still has the roll-out in their repertoire, but the timing is off. Instead of mid-fall, the roll-out happens after the thud, providing a convenient template for the chalk outline.

Interestingly, long after falling is a definite possibility, driving a motor vehicle is still in play. It's difficult to admit that your automotive pilot skills are waning, but it's a red flag when the bumpers on the car have more skid marks than a runway landing zone. Laws that govern traffic and travel are gradually viewed as suggestions. A late-stage commuter once asked me with a straight face, "Does the red light mean I need to stop, or are they stopping?" XL red flag!

Why don't I sense the need to adapt? Perhaps it's because, of the five primary senses, seeing and hearing lead the pack. While smelling, feeling, and tasting make life Uber-interesting, the ability to see and hear are primary to survival, yet seemingly the first to go on the journey to heaven. Corrective lenses for sight impairment are worn by people of all ages and often by people who don't need them, just for fashion. Wearing glasses to correct a sight deficiency isn't ordinarily perceived as a handicap, but strapping on hearing aids seems wrapped in late-stage sadness. Glasses are seen as accessories, while hearing aids are considered audio prosthetics. The typical friendly response, "I hear ya, man," is off the table. A deep regret settles in, fueled by the haunting truth that sitting in the second row of the Emerson, Lake, and Palmer concert in 1972 was the down payment on struggling to hear your grandchildren's piano recital. What pathetic irony that the high-pitched hearing aid squeal annoys everyone but the wearer. Nobody mentioned that the closing chapters come with white noise and tinnitus. Lip reading is the chief coping mechanism when life's soundtrack skips, which helps until everybody who talks to you is a medical provider wearing a mask. Eventually, I'll end up like a NASCAR vehicle that hit the wall out of turn three: still in the race, duct-taped together, leaking at the seams, and being lapped by the rookie drivers.

What can all this aging teach us? What's the low-hanging senescence truth? My takeaway is to interpret the disappearance of senses as the development of sensibility. The silence created by hearing loss creates quiet reflection, mainly reflecting on what I think the person said, which is often better than what they did say. Looking at life through "quad-focals" keeps me alert, entertained, and constantly startled by navigating without peripheral help. Thoughts about how life stinks get eliminated when the olfactory system goes on the fritz. May a growing sense of humor and gratitude outpace any senescent loss. That's all I have for now. I need to get to my tattoo appointment.

Chapter Seven

STUDENT BODY PREZ

"Too often we underestimate the power of
a touch, a smile, a kind word, a listening ear,
an honest compliment, or the smallest act of
caring, all of which have the potential
to turn a life around."
- Leo Buscaglia

The teenage years are unique in the continuum of growing up and growing old. One young adult author describes it as being on a bridge between childhood and adulthood...and the bridge is on fire. This transition period from childhood to adulthood often mixes the best and worst times. Great memories and lifelong friendships are built adjacent to heartbreak, disillusionment, and sometimes disaster.

For five consecutive years, I got invited by school districts in the United States and Canada to perform a 60-minute one-person show that was part stand-up comedy and part crisis intervention for senior high school audiences.

The show was built on the premise that a good laugh creates the possibility of a moment of honest introspection.

High school students are a beautifully complex bundle of charged emotions. While brilliantly creative and fun by appearance, they are exceptionally vulnerable, and many are facing challenges that can be overwhelming.

I started my presentation with observational humor and coming-of-age stories common to adolescence, like breaking curfew, learning to drive, and dating. This allowed me to reach out and build a rapport with my audiences; then, I ended by reaching out with an honest appeal to students who needed help to reach back. I knew that in every high school audience I was privileged to address, some students could be hiding a pregnancy, living in an abusive home, experiencing homelessness, or even contemplating violence or suicide.

Public schools have tremendous resources and personnel ready to assist students, but the counseling office is often used for academic more than actual help. The goal of my show was to be a catalyst for students to step out of hiding, identify their needs, and engage the school's intervention professionals.

And it worked. I had letters from Principals from all over North America letting me know that after my show, students were silently introspective and whispering privately to one another. One administrator called it "the quietest hour of the year." The quiet hour was followed by students making their way to the counseling office to admit their need for help.

Although I traveled throughout the academic year, the beginning of the new year was my favorite time to visit a campus. The return of the students from summer break meant a new beginning filled with possibilities. The optimism of a new year creates a tangible buzz. In my second year of touring, I went to Texas for the opening week of high school in the Dallas-Forth Worth districts.

On that sunny opening morning, I made my way to the sprawling campus of Plano Senior High School. Upon arrival, I checked in at the reception desk and found the Principal's office. She waved me in and jumped from her chair with a "Howdy! How y'all doing?" She warmly invited me to make my way down the hallway to the gymnasium to meet the student body president, who led the assembled students in the pledge of allegiance and then introduced me.

I trekked down the long hall, past the school's Wildcat logo on the floor adjacent to the wall of trophies behind glass. I turned into the vast gymnasium, brightly lit with all the bleachers pulled out in preparation for the twenty-five hundred students, and just in front of the first row of bleachers stood a microphone on a stand.

I approached the microphone and checked the audio signal with a "Testing, 1..2..3." While checking the acoustics, I saw a student looking into the gymnasium doorway. I put the microphone back to my lips and said, "Hey you. Come on in."

The student looked around, pointed to himself, and asked, "Who? Me?"

"Yes," I said, leaving the microphone on its stand and moving toward the doorway.

The student, dressed in jeans and a blue hoodie, cautiously entered the gym, head down as I asked, "Are you the student body president?"

"What? Me? No!"

"O.K. I thought you were. I mean, you look like the student body president to me."

"Yeah. Right. Really?" he shrugged.

"Yeah, I thought you were for sure; what's your name?"

"Kenny."

I looked him square in the eyes, reached out for a handshake, and said, "Hey Kenny, I'm Rick. Nice to meet you."

The bell rang, and students came running in from every direction. Teachers were pointing and yelling, and the stampede was on for the seats furthest from the floor.

The school's Principal jogged up and introduced the

Student Body President, who asked everyone to stand as he led everyone packed into the gym in the pledge of allegiance. In the brief chaos of everyone sitting down, he covered the microphone, turned toward me, and said, "Good luck."

Turning back to the 11th and 12th graders, he announced, "Today's speaker is from Seattle, Washington. Here are a few details about him. He got lost snow skiing in Switzerland and accidentally ended up in Italy. He won a ping pong tournament using his shoe as a paddle, saved the life of a guy choking on meatloaf, and played professional football for four hours. Please give Rick Enloe a Plano Wildcat welcome!"

The crowd erupted with applause as I strolled out to the microphone carrying my bag of props. I thanked the Student Body President for the kind introduction, then said, "It's great to be with you all today, and it is especially a treat to speak at the school my friend Kenny attends," I said, pointing to him on the front row.

I paused. Everyone looked down at Kenny, who smiled and gave me half a wave.

As in every school I performed, laughter in the first half of the performance stood in contrast to the silence at the end, where students were invited to be honest with themselves and ask for help.

As the students left the gym, they walked past me and thanked me, many reaching out for a fist bump or high five. The last student in the line out was Kenny. He stood opposite me. When he looked up through the hair hanging in front of his face, I saw a tear in the corner of his eye. He looked back down and said, "Thanks, Rick," and walked away, disappearing into the stream of students.

Therapists teach us that being seen is the first step to being heard and known. I call this process the cascade of acknowledgment. When someone sees you and calls out your name, it's like a waterfall, a beautiful outpouring of understanding that changes who you see in the mirror.

It's not a difficult thing to do.

I have no idea where Kenny is today. I don't know what he was carrying that day, and I'm not sure if my encounter caused him to question how he saw himself. I hope so. But I believe we are so often blind to what others can see in us. The only way we will begin to know is when they speak up. On the other hand, when we see potential or greatness in others, we carry the sacred trust to tell them.

To some extent, we are all like Kenny. At different points in our lives, we need someone to see something in us and call it out. Can you remember someone who paid attention to you and, in some small way, redefined how you saw yourself?

We all possess this incredible power to see potential in others and inspire them. On that September Monday in Texas, while I addressed the entire student body, I had a divine appointment with one student.

Keep your eyes open and your voice ready as you navigate each day for your Kenny moment--a moment of low-hanging truth.

Chapter Eight

8

WONDER WOMAN

"Depth of friendship does not depend
on length of acquaintance."
- Rabindranath Tagore

Edythe was all grown up when I met her.
After celebrating a birthday that put me solidly in mid-life, I realized that my closest friends were my age, with similar life experiences. We had all navigated formal educations, fallen in love, started families, experimented with facial hair, and grown our stomachs from six packs to full half cases. The passing of my Grandparents also contributed to a sense of living without sage advice or a trusted guide. My life seemed shiny but not significant, organized but inorganic. It was little wonder that I felt little wonder about the future. I decided that I needed to mix up my ethnically and economically homogenized relationships. So, I decided to intentionally seek out new friends who were older than me. Way older. I started asking around and searching for opportunities to meet

people who were over ninety. Most are women; many live in retirement homes that function like senior sororities.

I found one such community of older single women called the Ida Culver House on Ravenna Street. I contacted Beth, the lead social worker at the house, and asked if there was any possibility of volunteering. I mentioned that I had some experience in hospitality and organizing events. Beth was overjoyed. "One of our guests has been asking if we could organize a party for her friend whose 90th birthday is coming up. It would be wonderful if you could help us plan a celebration for her. Her name is Edythe. She lives alone in a house a few neighborhoods north of here but attends church with many ladies in our home. "

I pitched the idea to several of my friends, and we formed a birthday celebration committee. I interviewed Edythe's friends about what she might want for a birthday present. They said she loved bird watching and had several birdhouses on her patio. I remembered a birdhouse vendor at the local farmer's market and purchased a six-foot-tall bird condo with five different doorway holes and abundant perches. The party team decorated it with a big bow and a "happy birthday" banner. We set it up, front and center, in the multi-purpose room in Edythe's home church. Right next to the colorful birdhouse was a table holding up a cake with ninety candles.

Edythe was invited by her friend to a "women's ministry" meeting at the church but had no idea that she was the star of the show. She shuffled in, escorted by her friend, adorned in a colorful dress and matching hat, her purse on her elbow. We all cheered and sang happy birthday to her as she looked around joyfully. "You don't have anything better to do than this?" she asked with a wink. It was my first face-to-face encounter with Edythe, but her friends had prepared me for her quick wit and abrupt observations. It was an exceptionally entertaining event. Her surprise party jump-started a

fantastic twelve-year friendship between us. We became icon-
oclastic confidants with a 55-year age difference. She told
compelling stories and shared strong opinions. We talked for
hours over coffee and tea, exchanged book lists, enjoyed
lunch outings, and, over the years, shared concerns, fears, and
hopes. Edythe invited our entire family to her home many
times. We learned she didn't really live alone. She had an
extended family of cats, a backyard bird sanctuary, hundreds
of flowering plants (she could name every variety), and a
room full of dolls.

The dolls varied in size from a couple of inches to life-size.
Many of them were rare collectibles from the late 1800's. Some
had hand-painted porcelain faces with dresses trimmed in the
finest Belgian lace. The doll room was a converted bedroom
with cabinets and shelves on every wall. There were hundreds
of dolls.

One day, while enjoying a visit to her home, she guided me
more thoroughly through the doll room. During the tour, I
asked, "Which doll, out of all of these, is your favorite?"

Edythe immediately pointed to a collection of four small,
plain-looking dolls placed on a shelf at eye level.

"These? Why these?" I pressed.

"I made them, and I lost them," she noted in her matter-of-
fact style. "They started as brightly wrapped Christmas gifts for
my girls almost fifty years ago," she said, smiling.

She took the four dolls off the shelf, settled into her favorite
embroidered rocking chair in the living room, and began to
unfold the story behind her favorite quartet of dolls.

"In the fall of 1940, I poured wax into four doll head molds,
waited until it hardened, then hand painted the eyes and lips
on the wax faces. Then I stitched the doll bodies from hand-cut
patterns using old bed sheets for torso material," she recalled.

The meticulously constructed gowns for each doll came
from material scraps from her grandmother's fabric collection.

Each doll had a different outfit and hair color but similar facial features.

Edythe was also a writer. Her journals recorded the details of each step in the doll's design and construction, complete with sketches and material swatches, and the memories of the girls opening them on Christmas morning and dancing around the room. Her four girls treasured the handmade dolls but eventually joined the more extensive collection of dolls as they grew up and left home.

Twenty years later, during an extended holiday away, her house became a target of the growing phenomenon of home burglaries. Items stolen included electronics, jewelry, and collectibles, primarily dolls. The police eventually caught the neighborhood thieves and recovered some stolen property, including most of her dolls, except for the Christmas dolls.

Ten years after the robbery event, in the summer of 1970, Edythe found herself browsing an antique vendor in the middle aisle of the local mall. To her amazement, the four dolls were on sale in the glass display case.

"Those are my dolls!" she blurted out, pointing to the wax faces. "they were stolen from me."

The vendor turned and casually replied, "I'm sure you are mistaken," He disagreed.

"These are authentic handmade dolls from the Civil War era. We have traced the fabric to scraps of uniform material used by the Confederate army."

"That was my grandfather." Edythe supplied. "I have the bullet that they took from him at my house. See, I used scraps of material from my grandmother's notions. I molded the faces myself from a civil war era mold."

Unfazed by the volley of evidence, "There's no way, ma'am." said the dealer.

Edythe made a quick round trip to her house and returned to the mall's antique dealer within the hour. She brought her daily journal from 1940-1944 with sketches and material swatches from the doll's designer. She also had a picture of her grandfather in uniform and a small box lined with cotton, carrying a lead slug removed from his leg in the Civil War.

She laid the evidence on the counter and waited as the vendor slowly examined each item. He opened the journal and studied the entry for November 1940, where a sketch of each doll, with complete descriptions, filled the page.

"Wow! Amazing. I apologize. I can see now that these are your dolls. I can also see that they mean a great deal to you. You should buy them. They're one hundred fifty each, five hundred for the set," he insisted.

Edythe stared into the face of the vendor, then into the faces of the dolls, and made a decision. She bought the dolls and brought them back home.

"You bought back what belonged to you in the first place? " I clarified.

"They belonged to me. I made them," she said. "They didn't mean a thing to anybody else, but they meant everything to me," she said passionately.

Then, a tear formed in the corners of her eyes, "It's not any different than what God did for me. I was lost, and now I'm found-you know-amazing grace! I see that gospel truth when I see these dolls."

After hearing her story, I sat there staring at the dolls she held in her hands. Now that I understood their origin and journey of loss and redemption, they suddenly became beautiful to me as well.

Edythe's story of loss and redemption reflects the writings of poet John Donne's truthful verse;

"Twas much that man was made like God before, but that God should be like man much more."

Amen Edythe. Amen.

Chapter Nine

HOW AM I DRIVING?

"There is more credit and satisfaction in being
a first-rate truck driver than a tenth-rate executive."
- B. C. Forbes

No doubt, you've seen the bumper stickers, usually printed in yellow over black, inviting you to make a call and report or comment on how the driver of a commercial vehicle is performing. Most of us have never made the call.

These kinds of call-in programs, offered by various companies, are fleet monitoring risk management systems. The largest and oldest fleet monitoring enterprise in North America claims to have over 600,000 vehicles from 8,000 companies wearing the stickers on the back bumpers of commercial vehicles, which explains why we have all seen them. I encountered a truck one morning on my way to work that occasioned my only call-in experience.

I was driving down a four-lane road through the bustling

city of Bellevue, Washington. The King County road construction crew had placed bright orange cones and merge signs
warning drivers that the two eastbound lanes of Northrup
Boulevard were reduced ahead to only one lane, causing traffic
to merge into a long single-file line of slowly moving cars,
moving as ants headed to their hill in a rainstorm.

I entered the merge zone to bright red tail lights flashing
from the back of a truck in front of me as it slowed to a stop. I
didn't want to get squeezed by the eighteen-wheeled giant, so I
waited for the truck to merge into the single lane. Just then, I
saw the truck driver's arm politely waving me to proceed while
he waited to join me safely in the space behind me. I waved
appreciably and swerved to the left, navigating the narrow
passage.

As I signaled and maneuvered past the truck's rear bumper,
I noticed the sticker that said, "How Am I driving? Call 800-55-
DRIVE."

I lifted my voice over the adjacent sounds of construction
and said, "Hey Siri, call 800-55-DRIVE."

After a few seconds of silence, the operator answered
abruptly, "Your location, please?"

"Um... Northrup Way in Bellevue." I responded.

"Is the vehicle a van or truck?"

"A truck."

She shot back, "What's your complaint?"

"Well...I don't have a complaint," I reported smartly, "I have a
compliment. The driver was courteous and helpful."

There was an exaggerated pause.

"We don't have a category for that response, sir." She flatly
replied, sounding like I was wasting her time.

Puzzled, I asked, "What? Why not?"

"I don't have a category for a compliment, sir.

"You don't? Well...why don't you create a category?" I
reasoned out loud

"I can't. I don't have access to the program. This is a complaint system to track problems.

"Seriously? I mean...the bumper sticker asked 'how am I driving?' not 'How bad am I driving?"

Silence. Click.

I crept through the construction zone, thinking about what I had just learned from the toll-free complaint taker.

I imagined how draining it must be to sit at a desk all day and monitor complaints that identify problems needing solutions. "Business solutions" is a go-to mathematic marketing phrase for companies wanting to reduce risk and increase profits. Solving problems is sold as progress. It fits our analytic-mathematic tendencies, giving us a sense of control and promising an objective answer. There aren't two correct answers in math. We like that. So, delivery companies identify the packages on the truck as problems that delivery solves, while driving issues are addressed through surveillance and complaints.

Problem and solution. I hear those words every day.

Mathematic conversations abound! We hear about relationship, financial, workplace, and emotional problems. We are looking for solutions. Politicians promise to solve our societal problems if we vote for them. Education, religion, and proper nutrition are all touted solutions to our problems.

Track problems. Calculate solutions.

How many of us have been conditioned to operate personal complaint systems? We all have invisible yellow-on-black bumper stickers that say, "How Am I Doing? How Am I Parenting? How Good Am I at Life?" with social default settings that calculate and reduce each other to the lowest common denominator. We are frantically trying to find formulas for success. But then, like two lanes merging into one, we experience a moment of beauty that defies our programming. We share something beautiful, something complimentary, and it doesn't compute because beauty is art, not math. In a complaint-only system, there is no category for that kind of response. Trying to process art mathematically is like asking, "What's your favorite color between one and ten?

Maybe you've never heard of British author Dorothy Sayers. She died two years after I was born, but I wish I could have met her. She seems like an amazing person. You should google it up. She wrote poetry, articles, essays, and novels. Her mysteries keep company with Agatha Christy's classic crime-solving stories.

Do you remember that high school assignment to read Dante's Divine Comedy? That Italian poetic trilogy written in 1300, starting with Dante's trip to hell, called The Inferno.

"Not really," you say, "Why do you ask?"

Some critics consider Dorothy Sayer's translation of Dante's Divine Comedy her most significant contribution to literature. She's a big deal. Forty years before there were any bumper stickers on truck bumpers asking for complaints, she wrote,

"...the words problem and solution, as commonly used, belong to the analytical approach to phenomena and not to the creative." She continues, "The concept of problem and solution is as meaningless applied to the act of creation as it is when applied to the act of procreation."

Sayers explains that when a couple has a baby, they do not solve a problem. They produce a life. This blast from the past speaks to us today! She encourages us to live like a work of art to be displayed more than a math problem to be solved.

Sounds good, right? Who wouldn't rather live it up than always trying to add it up? For sure. But why, then, are we more attentive to complaints than compliments? Why do we give hurt more weight than hope? It's not that easy to break out of the problem-solution jail.

It doesn't mean we deny that there are problems to solve, but what if we begin to believe that life is more art than math?

What would change if we do more art and less math? Everything. When we stop solving and start shaping, there's no more reducing each other to the lowest common denominator. We could begin to see artistic layers of complexity and beauty in one another instead of monochromatic mathematics. Just as an artist mixes paint and broadcasts colors, life is better understood as a million brush strokes more than a long story problem.

Why not start by spending more time creating and less correcting?

Determine to pass along refreshing compliments more than broadcasting complaints.

Send the message: "You are a valuable work of art, and I'm glad you're on display!"

That's how to drive.

Chapter Ten

NEVER TRUST A TRICKSTER

"All those who believe in psychokinesis - raise my hand."
- Steven Wright

One of my favorite memories as a middle-school kid was going to the "Empire Magic and Novelty Shop" on Riverside Avenue in Spokane, Washington. Almost every other week, my friend Dave and I would ask his mom to drive us an hour from our small farming town in the country to shop for big-city novelties.

We had saved up our paper route money, arriving at the shop ready to spend it all on hilarious comic prizes like whoopee cushions, realistic-looking plastic vomit, and foot-long cigars. The store smelled like bubble gum and was dimly lit with black lights illuminating the dramatic posters on the back wall. The store proprietor would always reach out his hand and greet us with a buzzer shake, wearing a jester's hat and funny nose glasses. His name was Martin Gibson, and he owned the Empire, but he told us to call him "The Great Gibsy."

So we did.

His non-stop schtick would make us laugh so hard we could barely breathe as we paid for our big city entertainment collection. It was more than a novelty shop; it was Gibsy's Stage, and we were his willing audience.

Over time, we acquired all the gag basics, eventually graduating from rubber chickens to the fundamental magic trick essentials: coins and cards, scarves and balls for juggling, and all the sleight-of-hand tricks. We practiced our tricks, entertaining our families and friends at every opportunity.

The years stacked up, and eventually, we grew old enough to have middle-school children of our own. Stories of our exploits at the Empire never grew old, even though we did. Listening to the pitches and performances of The Great Gibsy remained foundational to our love of magic and magicians.

Then it happened.

Dave and I grew up, graduated high school, and went separate ways. Eventually, Gibsy passed away, and the Empire closed its doors on Riverside Ave. Over time, I landed a job at a local radio station in Seattle, Washington. I got a call from a production assistant at Bumbershoot, the city's biggest music, comedy, and arts festival. He asked if I'd like to introduce a world-famous Las Vegas magician act. I couldn't believe it. Gibsy was long gone, but I wanted to call and let them know that I had broken through to the big time.

The Vegas magic duo I was asked to introduce were renowned for amazing feats of illusion and magic and for featuring one tall magician who did all the talking. At the same time, his diminutive partner played the fall guy for every trick yet never said a word in the show.

When I arrived early at the venue on the day of the show, I was escorted through the stage door and greeted with a nod by the short silent magician. I was taken aback as he approached me and said, "Hi. Are you the one introducing us?"

"Yes," I said, stunned to hear the voice of the famously non-verbal entertainer.

"If you'd like to come backstage during the performance, you are welcome," he invited me.

"That'd be great," I said. Then, I began to wonder if his invitation was some farce. I could imagine these two tricksters suddenly calling me on stage during their act and asking me to step inside a phone booth that they would suddenly lock from the outside as it began to fill with water.

I remembered that Gibsy taught us to "never trust a trickster."

These two magicians were unique in another way. They got expelled from the official magician's association for "breaking the code." The code states that magicians should never explain or give away a trick for fear that people would lose interest in it and stop paying for magic shows. These magicians did not agree. They would perform amazing tricks, and then, when the audience was dazzled and mystified, they explained how it worked. So, strangely, it was honesty that distinguished these performers.

When they pulled away the curtains, turned on the lights, and showed how the trick played out, their full disclosure invited the audience into their sacred trust. Due to their forthright display, people felt drawn to believe that the tricks would ultimately not be at the expense of their naivety. Their truth-telling drew the audience together as confidants and participants instead of mere observers and suckers.

I have been thinking recently about this truth-telling-curtain opening phenomenon and how it can relate to our pressing societal challenges. We could all benefit from being drawn together in trust as long as our divisive and systemic bias remains a mystery, the less trust we have for the magicians in charge. When a trickster keeps you in the dark indefinitely, it opens the door to speculation and conspiracy, resulting in every audience member posting their version of how the trick works.

In contrast, the more they throw back the curtains, revealing clearly how and why these things are happening, the greater our confidence in the players on the main stage. We begin to see that "the code" is a fear-based survival narrative. It's fuel for the "fake it till you make it" school of thought. Concealment is terrible for personal relationships and even worse for public health. To paraphrase the Apostle John, "Full disclosure will set you free." How so? Because the veil of secrecy is as much a prison as a protection. Especially since selfish ambition is the only thing being protected.

There's some sweet, low-hanging truth when tricksters are willing to break the code.

Being included is the real magic.

ACT TWO

Chapter Eleven

11

TIN MAN

> "No, Oz never did give nothing to the Tin Man
> That he didn't, didn't already have."
> - Dewey Bunnell

L et me take you back to my days in sixth grade, where Mr. Gill, impeccably adorned in a blue pin-striped shirt and a red tie, ruled our classroom with an iron fist. He'd warn us about straying to his "bad side," painting a grim picture of a year we'd rather forget. He patrolled the room with a yardstick as his trusty sidekick, ensuring we all adhered to his strict code of conduct. It seemed like he saw us as soldiers in an army of obedience more than students in adolescence. He required that we sit up straight with our feet planted firmly on the ground.

I can still feel the sweat trickling down my back as I recall that fateful day at the end of our first week. His booming voice followed the sound of the last bell on Friday afternoon, "Everyone is dismissed today except for Mr. Enloe," he declared with a gaze that could freeze time. My friends vanished, leaving me alone to face the daunting Judge Gill. As I approached the bench, his question, "Do you know why I want to talk to you?" rang in my ears like a church bell.

"Am I on your bad side?" I squeaked, trying to play it cool. But he wasn't buying it. He slid my mediocre paper across the desk, fixing me with an incredulous stare over his reading glasses. "Did you write this, or did someone else write this for you?"

"I wrote it," I mumbled, feeling small and numb.

"Hmmm. That's difficult for me to understand because this writing is very average, and you are not. You are one of the most creative and intelligent students in this class, and this paper is neither. I expect you to teach me something, not just repeat what I taught you. You are a leader, and leaders don't do half a job. Rewrite this and bring it back Monday. You are dismissed."

I shuffled out, my ears burning and turning crimson to prove it. I spent the weekend researching, re-writing, and meticulously editing the paper. And something happened to me in the process. I started out being motivated by fear, not wanting to stand in front of the judge again, but his words kept racing through my mind as I worked. "One of the most creative and intelligent students...teach me something...you are a leader..." By the time I handed in my rewrite, I was more than a better writer. Something else had shifted within me. Slowly, the fear was replaced by confidence based on what he saw in me.

It's funny how we don't realize our worth until someone important points it out. I never saw myself as creative or intelligent until Mr. Gill painted that picture of me.

Over time, I also realized that I had learned from Mr. Gill a knack for seeing greatness in others but had never vocalized it.

I was reminded of Dewey Bunnell, the rockstar of the iconic band America, who hit the nail on the head with his song "Tin Man," referencing the Wizard of Oz character who didn't realize he had a heart until much later. I adapted his lyrics to my life, singing, "But Gill never did give nothing to the Rick Man that he didn't, didn't already have." When he pushed that paper back to me, I finally saw what I had all along.

And guess what? To this day, when a website asks me for security questions, I pick "Who was your favorite teacher?" and proudly type in Mr. Gill. He may have been tough as nails, but he helped me realize I was made of sturdier stuff. And, yes, you can probably hack me knowing that!

Chapter Twelve

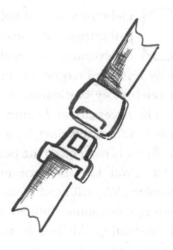

12

TRAVEL PHOBIA

"Avoiding danger is no safer in the long run than outright exposure. The fearful are caught as often as the bold."
- Helen Keller

C elebrating annual holidays often incorporates family gatherings, seasonal music, gift-giving, and the observation of timeless traditions. Most of these holiday festivities require an annual migration- either to home or a celebratory destination to join with others we know and love. The necessary and common component for the holidays is travel. When traveling long distances in short amounts of time, flying is most often the best option.

Air travel is a modern miracle, but not without some discomfort. We will need to wait in long lines, endure security screenings, encounter limited seating, and, for some, face fear and foreboding. All this to make our way to the appointed festivities and celebrations.

I have spent a significant amount of my adult life on

airplanes. I haven't set any air mileage world records, but my flight total is far beyond average. When you have years of experience at 35,000 feet, you end up with some unique experiences.

Nearly every holiday season, I end up sitting next to someone who is expressing nervous fear and anxiety about flying. The fear of flying is called acrophobia, based on the Greek word 'Akron,' which means summit or the highest point. This word is also the root of terms like acrobat to describe someone flying high or acropolis to identify the highest point in a city. This phobia is a significant holiday challenge for flight attendants trying to assist anxious passengers on their way to festive reunions. Recent polls indicate that on any given flight, seventeen percent of the passengers have some level of acrophobia. This means that an airplane with two hundred passengers has around thirty to forty people with sweaty hands, shortness of breath, or other manifestations of apprehensiveness.

If you happen to be the seventeen percent of air travelers with this fear issue, it doesn't help things to start your trip from a place called the "terminal" or hear public address announcements reminding you of a "final" boarding call. Words like terminal and final are straight out of the phobic narrative.

Therapists tell us that one component of anxiety is hyperawareness. Fear causes us to pay very close attention to details, a good response when truly in danger, but most often a disorienting experience on airplanes, especially the whole flight attendant warning sequence before take-off. The only people paying attention to the FAA's required safety briefing are the freaked-out 17 percenters. The last thing these apprehensive travelers need to hear are warnings and tragic possibilities.

"In the unlikely event of a water landing," they say.

To be prepared for the unlikely amphibian outcome, we are told that our seat bottom cushions "become" floatation devices, begging the question, "If they are going to "become" something, why not a center console Boston Whaler? "

Then we're told to pull the seat bottom cushion from beneath us and hold it to our chest. Having barely pulled off stowing luggage, this might be a less plausible maneuver. Plus, if hurling toward Earth at six hundred miles an hour, there's a good chance the seat bottom cushion has been freshly soiled, so I'm pretty sure we don't want to hug that.

Next, they announce that the cabin could lose pressure; if so, an oxygen mask will drop from the compartment overhead.

Then it gets complicated:

"Be sure to pull on the hose to start the flow of oxygen."

Sounds good, but in an emergency, it could be challenging to draw the line between pull and yank, severing the tube from the ceiling of the plane and rendering our life-giving mask useless.

"Oxygen will flow even though the plastic bag does not inflate."

Right.

"Put the mask over your nose and mouth and breathe normally."

I doubt anyone will breathe normally when the cabin goes pitch black and bags of snack mix fly through the cabin at warp speed.

When you hear, "Put your mask on before trying to assist others," it sounds like "Every man for himself." It's not too encouraging if you are someone who needs the assistance.

Sometimes, acrophobia is identified as a fear of heights, but if you think about it, it seems less about height and more about not staying at that height! In other words, it's fear of falling. It makes some sense that falling from a bicycle is not as frightening as falling from the sky, but the working definition of acrophobia is "an irrational fear of heights."

What does one do? We all, phobic or not, should immerse

ourselves in factual information about air travel, starting with the most profound truth: flying is the safest way to travel. Commercial air travel records indicate only one fatality for every billion miles traveled. By comparison, there are seven fatalities per billion miles traveled by car (and over 200 fatalities per billion traveling on a motorcycle).

How contrarian! The data indicates we are most afraid of what is safest. Yet, it's strange that knowing these facts does not (in fact) cancel fears. If facts did inform our fears, we should fear driving, right? But most people I question say driving feels safer because we are in control.

So, giving up control means trusting someone else with our well-being. Somehow, we equate and attribute greater risk to greater trust. At least, we might think we have no one to blame but ourselves.

Ultimately, it's not the hard data that helps us manage our holiday travel fears; it's our internal homing devices. Like the millions of birds that migrate to their seasonal homes, we muster the courage to push back on the irrationality of our feelings and demonstrate the brave willingness to take on the fear and risk, following our instinct to gather where we belong. The nest seems safe, but we were all born to soar.

We find low-hanging comfort and inspiration as we are willing to trust others for our safe arrival. We must remember that we are not alone; ours is always a shared journey. Bon Voyage.

Chapter Thirteen

13

NEIGHBOR GUY

"I want you to be concerned about your next-door neighbor.
Do you know your next-door neighbor?"
- Mother Teresa

For over half a century, the late Fred Rogers continued asking, "Won't you be my neighbor?" Most of us who watched Mr. Rogers felt like we knew him; like we were his neighbor. That is more difficult to replicate in day-to-day life with our actual next-door neighbors.

Recent data from the Pew Research Center indicates that the younger one is, the less likely they are to know their neighbors. Even for the older set, those sixty-five and beyond, the study discovered only one-third claim they 'mostly' know who their neighbor is.

The research results indicate rural communities are better than urban dwellers at knowing their neighbors, but surprisingly, it didn't change how much people interact with their neighbors. Knowing someone doesn't mean hanging out with them.

After reading the Pew Research Center neighbor report, I decided to buck the societal trend by getting to know my neighbor and doing something together. Like most of us, I knew what my neighbor looked like. I would occasionally wave at him as he drove by my house, and sometimes, we would say a quick hello when we found ourselves at the side-by-side mailboxes at the end of the block.

We had lived as neighbors for five years, and I referred to him as "the guy next door" whenever I saw him. One day, I found an advertisement for fishing equipment addressed to the guy next door in my mailbox. I noticed his first name was Guy. The guy next door was the Guy next door!

As I closed the mailbox, I saw him in his front yard, so I walked over and said, "Guy, I found your fishing catalog in my mailbox."

He walked over to the fence, grabbed the catalog I was extending in his direction, and said, "Hey, thanks."

I seized the neighborly opportunity and said, "So, you're a fishing....guy?"

He grinned and said, "Yeah, I like fishing but haven't gone since I'm between boats."

I figured he'd seen my boat in the driveway occasionally, so I said, "I'm going to drag some bait around this weekend if you want to go."

Without hesitation, he said, "I'd love to. Let me know what time and what to bring."

I told him not to worry about anything; I'd bring all the gear and some food for us both. The following Saturday morning, he crossed the street wearing a bucket hat and a khaki fishing vest and jumped in my truck with the boat behind it.

On the way to the boat launch, I asked him where he'd

fished and what kind of bait he used, and he asked me about the boat; things were cordial, and I was learning about where he'd grown up and what he did for work.

Once we were off the dock with our lines in the water, after opening the ice chest and popping open a couple of cool drinks, he turned to me and said, "O.K. What? What are you selling?"

Taken back a bit, I asked, "What do you mean selling?"

He sipped and grinned, "Well, you caught me in a situation where I can't go anywhere, so I figured you wanted to pitch me something."

I grinned back, "No, I'm here to catch a fish, not you. I just figured it was wrong that we have been neighbors for five years and don't know anything about each other."

"Oh."

"Yeah, that's it," I assured him, "So what's your story?"

He looked down for a few seconds, then lifted his head and said, "You see this scar on my cheek?"

I honestly hadn't noticed it until he pointed it out.

"Ten years ago, I put a gun to my head and pulled the trigger. That's where I got this scar."

Wow.

"No way!" I whispered, wide-eyed.

I was expecting to hear about where he was born and how many siblings he had or some essential backstory, but I couldn't believe he started by describing a suicide attempt.

"I figured when you saw the scar, you knew," he confessed and looked down.

Like I said, I hadn't even noticed the scar.

So he was thinking that he knew what I was thinking. But I wasn't.

How many times do we tell ourselves that everybody can see our regrets? The truth is, we're the only ones who do.

He went on to tell me about lost hope and how he talked himself into believing everyone would be better off without him around. Then he looked down and said, "As soon as I pulled the trigger, I wanted to take it back, and when I woke up in the hospital, I couldn't believe it. Every day since has been such a gift."

Then he lifted his head, and he looked different to me.

He hadn't visibly changed, but in that honest moment, I invisibly had.

I agree with renowned poet Maya Angelou, who said, "I think we all have empathy. We may not have enough courage to display it."

When Guy was willing to risk vulnerability, he invited me to walk into his history and summoned my courage to empathize. It was a precious gift. Therapists often call this the "gift of going second." When someone is willing to go first, telling the truth opens the "me too" door to authenticity. I experienced it that day.

I thanked him for trusting me with his truth. Our conversation gave way to the sound of the incoming tide slapping against the hull, and then he broke the silence and asked me about my history. We told stories all afternoon, casting bait and spinning reels and tales. We never got a bite, but we both caught a glimpse of the humanity that lives inside the houses across the street. His vulnerability still strikes me. He had accepted my offer, and I was given the gift of offering my acceptance.

I realized what Fred Rogers had been saying all those years. One afternoon, together on the water, the neighbor at the mailbox was no longer just a guy; he was Guy, my friend. Sometimes, you'd be surprised when you ask someone across the street or the fence, "Won't you be my neighbor?"

The low-hanging truth in this experience applies beyond

next-door neighbors. People who are rich in relationships maintain a healthy curiosity and generous spirit in every context. Never underestimate the power of a sandwich, a fishing pole, and an invitation to others.

Chapter Fourteen

14

CRUMB AND QUEEN

"A computer once beat me at chess,
but it was no match for me at kick boxing."
- Emo Philips

U ntil recently, two things were true about the two of us in our present household:

1. Our knowledge and interest in sourdough bread was strictly related to ingesting it.

2. Neither one of us had ever played chess.

The now-elapsed global pandemic has changed all of that. Once it became clear to us that we were going to be at home for most of a year, we took on the ultimate double challenge:

Learn how to make sourdough bread.

Discover how to compete on the chess board.

So, we learned and discovered.

We baked and baked and baked.

And we castled and checked and check-mated.

We played chess in the gaps between folding the dough, pre-shaping the loaf, and lining our Dutch oven with parchment. We baked and played poorly at first, but with each loaf and each contest, we realized how much sourdough and chess could provide life lessons beyond the oven and the board.

First, the sourdough journey.

If they wander down the bread-baking trail, most people will start with a typical yeasted no-knead artisan bread. If all goes well, the baker can put things in another gear, change lanes, and go for the trophy loaf: Sourdough.

A perfectly baked slice of sourdough bread is for many a gastronomic delight. Sourdough is renowned for its iconic tangy flavor, dewy crumb, and crisp, crackly crust.

My Sourdough "Bon Appetite" top five: (It is probably not a good idea to read my top five when hungry.)

A piece of sourdough hand-torn from the loaf and slathered in Irish butter.

A toasted slice of fresh sourdough topped with blackberry freezer jam.

Sourdough croutons dipped in top-shelf cold-pressed extra virgin olive oil.

Sourdough slices under the broiler, topped with grated parmigiano-reggiano.

A toasted cheese sourdough sandwich made with extra sharp cheddar on the panini grill.

Like the bread, the low hanging truth is baked into the journey.

SOURDOUGH LESSON ONE: *The Starter*

Sourdough is a slow-fermented mixture that rises and develops based on a natural leavening agent instead of a commercial yeast. It's called the sourdough starter. Our starter was a gift from our friend Suzanne. It felt like we were adopting a child more than receiving a creamy white fermented culture.

The starter is everything. It must be fed, rested, managed, and treasured. Once the starter is fed with flour and water, it develops air bubbles and expands. When it doubles in size, we check the buoyancy of the dough by putting a drop of starter in a glass of water. If the elixir floats, it's ready to add the salt, water, and flour mixture that makes the tasty sourdough loaf.

Timing the bake depends on "catching it on the rise." If the starter is actively expanding after being fed, the starter is sending the message to begin the process of developing the dough for baking.

This is the first life lesson of the sourdough starter: success (expanding and rising) depends on knowing how to nurture the starter. For instance, when starting a new day, it is always best to feed our souls and wait quietly for hope and faith to rise in preparation for the crucible of our challenges.

Feeding the starter is a philosophical exercise when starting a new project or relationship. Most of us stop and think before we do something, but the "sourdough philosopher" in us says, "Think again." It's not the initial thoughts but the exercise of patient re-thinking that allows us to "catch it on the rise" that makes something meaningful and valuable. In both baking and comedy, timing is everything. Waiting for the right time to start is as important as any other ingredient.

SOURDOUGH LESSON TWO: *Developing the dough*

When the starter is ready, we place our big bowl on a scale, zero it out, and add warm water, organic flour, and sea salt to make the dough. Once the dough is mixed, we start the seven-hour process of folding it over at intervals to develop its characteristic taste and texture. You get the feeling that the dough would prefer to be left alone instead of disturbed and pulled apart every couple of hours.

How many of us have that same predisposition? We prefer to live undisturbed, but that's not how life works. Herein lies the second low-hanging sourdough truth: when we are stretched, we develop character. Real life happens when we combine all the ingredients: the kids and jobs, the bills and sickness, and stress. As we experience the pulling, bending, and inconvenience, we learn to persevere, allowing our lives to develop taste and texture. Don't give up! This is the necessary development stage. It doesn't last forever and is a prelude to the fantastic aroma to come.

*SOURDOUGH LESSON THREE: **Half-baked is not baked.***

When the dough has been folded and pulled for hours, the loaves are shaped (we use oval proofing baskets with linen liners) and rested before baking. We heat our oven to 450 degrees and score the dough with a straight, giving it a distinctive design and toasted "ear" when it is done. (BONUS TRUTH: the scar from being cut later becomes the loaf's unique signature and admired feature. To quote a friend of mine, "Let your wounds become windows.")

We put the loaf onto a parchment paper and into a covered Dutch oven for the first twenty minutes. When the timer goes off, we take the cover off the Dutch oven to reveal the half-baked loaf. We can see what the bread will look like, but it needs more time in the heat to be ready. It's visible but not edible.

How often have we heard someone say, "It was a half-baked idea" or "A half-baked scheme for getting rich?" There's some low-hanging truth in knowing the value of fully baking our ideas. There is no shortage of half-baked notions in our world today. Most of them are perpetuated by half-baked hucksters who are working a half-baked scheme for getting rich.

When our ideas are not fully baked, they need a second baking. The second baking is hotter than the first. No lid. It's the heat that brings out the character of the loaf and the artistry of the scoring. To transform an adage, "If you can't stand the heat, you'll end up half-baked."

It's little wonder why the holy grail of baking is sourdough.

There's a lot to do.

It matters how you do it.

AND NOW, let's play some Chess!

Who knew there were all different kinds of chess? We learned the Western or International Chess game, which comes from 15th-century southern Europe. It is unique from other "chess-ish" games in the Far East, like xiangqi in China or janggi played in India.

A standard Western Chess set has 32 total pieces. That's 16 chessmen per side. The starting place of each piece mirrors the opponent, with the most powerful pieces on the back line.

The total collection of pieces is often referred to as 'material.' If you want to sound astute while losing, say, "Wow. I am experiencing a drain on my material," which sounds so much more stately than "I hope you face serious injury for taking my queen with your sleeper knight!"

Although basic chess is not over-complicated, the option to do a deep dive and never be heard of again exists. It's that deep. Have you ever heard of the Shannon Number? The Shannon Number, named after the American mathematician Claude Shannon, represents all possible move variations in chess. Shannon postulates that the number of possible chess games exceeds the number of atoms in the observable universe!

Mind blown.

At this point, we are just getting our 'Chess legs' so the number of atoms in the universe can relax, but we have learned some life lessons from this most challenging game.

Here's some of what the Queen of Games has taught us:

CHESS LESSON ONE: You cannot begin without moving (and it must be forward).

Pawns are the most common chess pieces, with eight pawns per side. While they are common, they are vital. On the back row, behind the pawns, are the knights, the pieces that look like horse heads. The knight is the only piece that can jump over a piece in front of it. As a result, knights and pawns are the only pieces that can be moved to begin a game. When you think about starting something new, the opening moves are crucial to the success of any endeavor. Figure out what can be done and focus on those moves.

It's not called a chess sit; it's called a chess move.

When you do move, move with purpose. If you wait for someone else to determine your next move, it's likely to have an unintended outcome. Grab the steering wheel immediately and keep driving until you get there.

CHESS LESSON TWO: Stay out of your own way.

One of the crucial facets of any opening move is to create lanes for the powerful pieces on the back row to access the board and impact the game. It's possible to be indecisive and block yourself from your powerful but trapped potential.

Don't be afraid to lose some ground to win what matters most. A big part of chess strategy is the willingness to sacrifice certain pieces for a better position in the game. In chess, as in life, sacrifice is necessary. We all have to give something up to get something else.

Don't get fooled by thinking there's a formula. Chess is a reactive game more than it is a strategic game. The best players don't let what's probable blind them from what's possible.

CHESS LESSON THREE: Every threat is an opportunity.

Your opponent is out to eliminate you, but you have all the material you need to flip the script and turn an attack into an advantage. We never improve unless we are willing to compete with someone who has a better game. Don't be afraid to lose to learn. Small advantages add up. Covering one more square or defending another piece pays dividends when the action heats up.

THESE ARE JUST a small collection of low-hanging Queen and Crumb truths, collected after more than a year in competition. While nobody likes to lose and everybody wants to win, it is necessary to navigate those outcomes in the context of marriage carefully.

Perhaps the reason that the Victorian elite sat at opposite ends of monstrously large dinner tables was likely tied to the chess games played before dinner. For a few hours, the emotional commitment made to a chess game can temporarily overshadow wedding vows.

We're also pretty sure the saying, "To the victor go the spoils," was uttered by a husband describing his disheveled meal after a strong endgame at happy hour. We found out that there is a certain "lack of receptivity" by the losing party. If the winner happens to compliment the loser on a particular move, it gets interpreted as "Nice try, loser." We advise a long walk and a few hours of silence after a hard-fought match, followed by a cup of tea and a buttered slice of fresh sourdough bread.

The low-hanging truth we found in making bread and

playing chess demonstrates the power of things timeless over things trendy. There is nothing wrong with flawlessly shredding on Guitar Hero's Dragonforce's in 18 hours chunks, but we'll take a Ruy Lopez opening with a cup of tea and slice of sourdough over a screen flooded with lights, wandering like dark souls into treacherous online labyrinths. Real-time creating and competing delivers what screen time cannot!

Chapter Fifteen

BIG GUY GROCER

"I found there was only one way to look thin:
hang out with fat people."
- Rodney Dangerfield

I have always enjoyed grocery shopping. Some people do not, but I look forward to it. I think of a trip to the market as an adventure followed by an art project. The adventure part includes discovering what is fresh and available in each season. The artistry ensues when I get back home, don my chef's jacket, tell Alexa to "play Bach," and launch into preparation, followed by a presentation that leads to the reward of sharing a meal.

Some key details drive my enjoyment of gathering groceries. First, I only shop for food items. I appreciate others in my household who buy necessities like detergents, paper products, or health and beauty necessities, but I enjoy focusing on edibles. Secondly, I am not a bulk purchaser; I shop daily. I learned the joy of daily shopping while living in Europe for a year. The rhythm of each week included daily visits to procure ingredients. I anticipate arriving at the bakery early on Saturday mornings for fresh baked bread and pastries. On Mondays, I would visit the butcher shop and the open market on Thursday afternoons--the days in between, to the grocery store to fill in the menu gaps.

As such, my local grocery store plays a crucial role in my overall sense of culinary delight. I rarely arrive at the store with a list or a meal plan. I'll start at the meat and fish counter if I feel carnivorous. I peruse the available proteins, and my choice becomes the meal's foundation, surrounded by complementary sides. If I am in the vegetarian mood, I'll circle the produce aisle, considering how I could pair edamame, zucchini, or mushrooms with a polenta or garlic risotto. I like to allow the best available products to direct my imagination.

Like I said, I looked forward to grocery shopping...until recently. The store manager has greeted me at the door for the last couple of months by saying, "Hey, Big Guy." I'm not trying to be oversensitive or gloomy, but his greeting takes the zest out of my previously joyful shopping experience.

To be fair, the manager is a good grocer. The reason I shop at the store he manages is precisely because it is managed well. And, true, I am a person of above-average size. I stand six foot three and weigh in the mid-two hundreds, so comparatively speaking, I am bigger than he is. I also know that "Big Guy" can be a term of endearment like "Buddy" or "Dude." Given all that, I am facing a "volume value" greeting on the way into a market where I purchase items that could contribute to my future circumference. It's ruining my art project.

He says, "Hey, Big Guy," and I hear, "Hey, Oversized Human" or "Hey, Morbidly Obese Man." It makes me think, "I probably shouldn't eat today," or "I wonder if my shirt could be used as a jib sail on a small schooner?"

Part of the "Big Guy Challenge" is the difficulty of what to say in return. So far, I sit with shame, say "hi," and walk on. But lately, I've been thinking about responding with "How's it going, Tiny?" or "Hello, my petite friend." Miniature poodles are called "toy poodles," but "toy grocer" doesn't have the same ring, so maybe there's nothing there. But I realize that retaliatory labeling wouldn't change anything. Plus, being reminded that I'm large doesn't necessarily constitute a comeback. It's a state-ment greeting, not a question greeting. Question greetings like "How's it going?" invite a response, but a statement greeting, "Hey, You are Enormous," stands on its own. Even if you say it like a question, "Hey...Big Guy?"-it's rhetorical. Still, the truth hurts. It seems mean-spirited, like greeting a Parkinson's patient with "What's shakin' Dude?" or welcoming a bald guy with "Yo! Slick." (Everybody knows "Yo" is short for "Yolk.")

I wonder if I am supposed to take a stand next time I get "Big Guyed" before it becomes a slippery slope and the greeter starts to go off on others. How bad would I feel if I overheard him greeting pick-up truck owners with, "S'up Cooter?" or pointing to someone excessively manicured and yelling, "Nailed it!" from the impertinent grocer?

You're probably thinking, "Hey, Big Guy, you don't have to put up with this; just go to a different store."

I thought about it and decided I didn't want to. This is by far the best vendor of quality ingredients in my area. Why should my world become smaller because of a simple body image slur?

So, I made a decision.

The only answer is to lean into it. Just go with the stereo-type and reinforce the stigma of being super-sized. No messing around. I stroll into the store, large head up, owning that I'm not coming in sporting a six-pack; I'm going out with one. My puffy fingers proudly grab the heavy cream to finish the Mornay sauce that anchors my future shepherd's pie. I flex my stout bicep and toss that Cambozola cheese into the basket, a perfect compliment to the Oregon Pinot Gris.

And suddenly, I realize the genius of the greeting. The insightful grocery manager knew I would eventually come to peace with the roly-poly greeting by buying more products. He knew it would stir up my portly pride, and I would fight for the right to be huge.

It worked! Now I look forward to the "Hey Big Guy" greeting, and I've never eaten so well!

Chapter Sixteen

ON A ROLL

"The best way to find out what we really need
is to eliminate what we don't."
- Marie Kondo

In ancient Greece, the high point of fashion might have
been the Toga, but geographically, the highest elevation
in any city was called the Acropolis. That word means
city summit. Generally, the top of the highest hill served as a
tribute to the patron god of that city. Most famously, the
Parthenon is a temple to the Athena on the Athens Acropolis.

The hilltops or city summits were also centers of the
community's commercial and social life. Whether Epicurean or
Stoic, the philosophers preferred these lofty locations for their
elevated conversations.

With this in mind, I began to think about the highest point
in my city. I live in a harbor town, where the main street starts
at sea level. One location sits high above the harbor, over-

looking the marinas and lighthouse below. This is our acropolis.

Sure enough, there is a magnificent structure on the highest point in town, brightly lit and surrounded by hundreds of shopping chariots. This building may be missing the classical Corinthian columns, but it serves as the gathering place of those devoted to Lord Kirkland, patron God of the Costco membership warehouse club.

Like the ancient Greek temples, our Costco is a thriving commercial, social, and philosophical place to shop, eat, and gather.

Lord Kirkland is the fifth largest retail force in the Consumption Pantheon, dwarfed by Lord Amazon, but still a formidable source of happiness and havoc, leading all others in the sale of wine. His provisions include a vast array of over 4,000 different items to buy, but beyond all, he is undeniably the master vendor of toilet paper. Over one billion rolls of Kirkland toilet paper are sold per year.

Worldwide, nearly 250,000 servants of Kirkland work around the clock to orchestrate his offerings.

Approaching the Temple of Kirkland is very much like traveling internationally. To enter, one must show their membership passport, and after shopping, receipts must be examined by the customs officer at the door to ensure you have paid proper duty.

Once inside Kirkland's agora, the executive, business, and gold star members stroll carts past each other while sampling morsels of the marketplace-warmly offered by servants wearing the Costco smock, a play on the traditional Greek toga, also adorned in hair and beard nets. Each store is organized around a common space, where Kirkland's followers can consider purchasing from tables of neatly folded designer clothing. The possibility of attending a future civic event and seeing the shirt you are wearing on hundreds of others becomes an exhilarating possibility.

Lord Kirkland's Costco is unique to other consumer temples in the sheer variety of items. Where else can you get an eye exam, then buy a forty-pound vat of Mac-n'cheese and a living room sectional in one setting?

The variety of items often causes a purchasing condition known as Costco vertigo. This purchasing confusion leads even the most experienced consumer to choose products that should not be purchased together. For instance, it is not uncommon to see someone at the check stand, swirling with Costco vertigo, paying fifty dollars for a cholesterol-reducing medicine, then taking ten steps to procure a classic $1.50 Kirkland Jumbo hot dog. This condition blocks the pathways in the brain that would ordinarily know that a commitment to a four-foot wheel of cheese eliminates the need to stockpile toilet paper.

The sheer size of the Costco products can pose a challenge as well. Is it even possible to responsibly use a fifteen-pound box of turmeric? I can imagine, upon my death, an appointed executor reading my last will, "Being of sound mind and body, I bequeath the remaining ten pounds of turmeric in equal amounts to my surviving children and their heirs."

Due to the warehouse sizing of Costco items, buying a personal, romantic gift in Kirkland's domain is challenging. Seldom would someone of interest be pleased with a 55-gallon barrel of perfume or a slinky nightgown that says Kirkland across the front.

One of the most unusual items for sale is the Costco casket. It seems practical for the long-term estate planner, but storing it inconspicuously from its future users gets tricky. "Don't worry about it, Grampy; it's just a big toolbox I got to organize the garage. Wink wink."

Another unique feature of Kirkland's realm is the choice of impulse items near the check stand. Most brick-and-mortar retailers have small items near the register to add to your shopping, like gum or batteries. Not so in Costco. "Will that be all today? Uh, no, let's throw in that ski boat."

The most devoted Kirkland followers are well on the way to creating a miniature version of Costco at their homes. Garages across the city begin to resemble the store's remote regions, where bottled water cases serve as a base for the stacks of paper towels, toilet paper, and boxes of tissues. Freezers are packed with ready-made entrees, and pantries house buckets of unsalted nuts nestled tightly beside the turmeric box. The yearning for a Toga grows stronger.

We will slowly begin to resemble what we worship. Herein is the low-hanging truth.

What could the Palace of Consumption provide in the future? Day surgery? Sports betting?

How about adoption services?

"Your baby is cute; what's his name?"

"Kirk."

Chapter Seventeen

JAVASCOPE™

"I don't believe in astrology;
I'm a Sagittarius, and we're skeptical."
- Arthur C. Clarke

The original inspiration came to me on a rain-soaked and foggy Monday morning in Seattle. I drove out of the garage onto Interstate 90 for the first ten miles of my trip to work. My bicycle was strapped to the rack on the back of the car for the second half of the commute. I navigated to an empty parking spot on Mercer Island. I wore water-resistant pants and a jacket with my work clothes in the sealed pantry hanging on my bike's rear rack. I clipped on my helmet, uncoupled my cruiser from the car rack, and embarked on the second half of my commute. I put my head down and made the twelve-block ascent up Fourth Avenue to Denny Way when I saw the open sign on a new coffee shop adjacent to my building. I swerved onto the sidewalk and pulled my bike onto a covered patio. After locking my two-wheeled transport to the bike stand, I removed my helmet and stepped into the warm, fragrant space where a cheerful barista asked me what I'd like to drink.

I looked up to the daily special board and noted that the day's coffee was from the Robusta variety and was described as "full-bodied, bold, smoky with a hint of satire."

It was a perfect description of me (especially the full-bodied part), so I said, "I'll have the special; it's my signature bean"- (even though I didn't know beans about beans at this point.)

I sat on a long table of coffee sippers in the only empty chair. I glanced at the lady across the table and noticed she was engrossed in reading her daily horoscope from the freshly printed Seattle Times. I had a casual awareness of astrology but had never seriously considered the stars a source of guidance. On the other hand, she seemed to be a serious student of the zodiac's daily predictions.

As I sipped the crema off the top of my caffeinated elixir, I wondered if the beans were trying to tell me something. I stared into the velvety blackness in the cup, and the idea shot through my brain like a cappuccino foamer.

I began to ponder, what if life's answers were revealed in the beans instead of the stars? What if instead of looking to a horoscope, this lady needed to find her Javascope™?

I soon discovered the Twelve Beans of the Joediac.™ I pushed on the information like a French press at sunrise and began to see how the beans offer more profound advice on life's journey than the twelve stars of the Zodiac. I felt like the beans roasting could be more cosmically significant than the stars rising!

Had I percolated one of the most remarkable insights since the Industrial Revolution? (OK...maybe that's a stretch, but my feelings make sense if you consider that I conceived of the Javascope™ while drinking an Ethiopian blend that carries twice the caffeine of most other beans!)

Since that pivotal mind grind, I have been on a quest to help people understand how the Javascope™ speaks to human thriving and the pursuit of a good life.

Understanding how to harness the power of the Javascope™ is easy.

First, everyone is born under a specific bean. Your birth month determines your life path and correlates directly with the bean harvested that month.

Secondly, the bean you were born under blends most perfectly with other specific beans, making the Javascope™ essential in selecting life partners. The outdated astrological pickup line, "Hey Baby, what's your sign?" will soon be replaced with the more evolved "Hey Sugar, what's your bean?"

For instance, the Sumatran bean profile marked everyone born in May. Their lives exude earthy tones and low acidity, yet they have decadent tendencies. The mellow aspects of the May Sumatrans blend nicely with Robusta varietals, adding some spice and intensity to these sweet beans.

The Javascope™ for this group would include a Daily Bean Alert™ regarding major purchasing decisions between 5 and 9 am Los Angeles time as well as a weekly Perk Prediction™ such as "You may find yourself pleased with an unexpected pour over windfall or advantage in a negotiation. Keep an eye out for an unusual conversation with someone in authority. Filter your thoughts regarding politics and religion to maintain a smooth aftertaste."

The Javascope™ has proven to provide great insight into your health, romance, and career choices. Life will always put you in hot water; allowing that to steepen, drip, and extrude your best self is up to you. You never know when you might get a Double Shot™ of good fortune! So many people live their lives trying to avoid taking any heat. Still, when you lean into the beans, you understand that roasting brings out your character and develops the subtle, distinctive, and tasteful nuances that make you unique.

The twelve beans of the Joediac™ are the most reliable source of inspiration and innovation without doubt. Don't be a "doppio" and spend your time looking to the stars when the beans are dripping with timeless wisdom -one cup at a time. Be the first one in your circle of friends to admit that you don't wake up to drink coffee; you drink coffee to wake up.

This low-hanging caffeinated truth raises several questions:

Is an addiction to the beans better than a devotion to planetary movement?

Are the beans the final revelation or just the next step on our path to enlightenment as we espresso our need for insight?

Is this what it takes to finally survive the daily grind?

I say something is brewing and it's "bean" a long time coming.

Chapter Eighteen

CHOKED UP

"A dogmatic belief in objective value is
necessary to the very idea of a rule which is not
tyranny or an obedience which is not slavery."
- C. S. Lewis

B efore having children of our own, we followed the
path of least resistance and acquired a dog. In
choosing our canine companion, we disregarded wise
counsel and breeding tendencies and made the selection based
solely on cuteness.

We selected an adorable Cairn terrier and named him
Roscoe.

The Cairn terrier breed originated in the Scottish Highlands and gained notoriety by playing the part of Toto in the
original Wizard of Oz movie. The Cairn was considered a
working dog; however, in our experience, the working part has
been passed on to the owner over time. Dog specialists
consider the Cairn terrier to be "energetic." Our Roscoe was

exceptionally energetic in destroying most of our possessions and some of our friendships.

He energetically ripped the headliner out of our car and shredded the floor-to-ceiling curtains in my sister's house while scratching and clawing holes in any wall or door that separated him from the Scottish Highlands. He barked several million times daily, dismembered house plants, and pursued a romantic relationship with our couch pillows. He growled at everyone, peed on everything, and rarely slept. But he was adorable.

It occurred to me that he possessed a substantial gift of disobedience. As the human and owner, I realized his redemption was in my hands. I asked a veterinarian for advice and signed Roscoe up for canine obedience classes. I contacted the confident obedience class leader, who firmly instructed me to show up at the appointed time with my disobedient best friend and a ten-foot leash equipped with a choke chain collar.

Roscoe's regular collar was strictly ornamental. It had a happy, sparkly vibe. The clip designed to connect a leash had only been used to dangle his custom name tag and vaccination information metal. The two attachments made a rhythmic clanging sound whenever he ran around. When the clanging stopped, usually something was being chewed to oblivion. The choke chain collar was entirely different. The only sound it made was the quick zipper-like warning when pulled on by the human, followed by the dog's curious inability to breathe.

On the day of our first class, I loaded Roscoe with his new leash and choke chain collar into the car, arriving at an open field between two buildings. A total of a dozen dogs were in our class, including eight Rottweilers, two pit bulls, a Doberman pincer, and Roscoe the Cairn terrier.

The instructor gathered us into a large circle and explained our first exercise. Our gathering circle became a sniff-fest. Dogs have 30,000 scent capabilities, and 28,000 are tuned to the

smell of other dog's caboose. After exhaustive leashing by the
human members of the group, we settled into the instructions.
As I listened intently, my eyes darting around the circle of fierce
classmates, I felt an unusual sensation on my right ankle. I
looked down, and Roscoe was lifting his leg and finding relief
at the expense of my right shoe. I pulled the leash straight up
and engaged the choke chain while lifting Roscoe off the
ground. He landed back on the ground with gagging and
coughing sounds. The entire class started barking and lunging
in our direction. The journey to obedience was on!

We were instructed to walk in a circle, counter-clockwise,
keeping our dogs adjacent to our left shoulders. Should the dog
stray from the appointed position, pull quickly on the choke
chain collar until the student returns to the sweet spot,
releasing all tension on the leash to the collar. The big idea was
to make one space comfortable and all other places uncomfort-
able. As I walked slowly, Roscoe began to run ahead, so I let out
the full extension of the leash, and when he reached the ten-
foot line, I pulled up and back quickly. Roscoe shot off the
ground, passed me at shoulder level, and landed behind me
but directly in line with an oncoming junk-yard Doberman.
The Doberman's owner was surprised by the sudden lurch
forward of his dog preparing to make an appetizer out of the
bite-sized terrier. The sudden sound of vicious barking startled
everyone in the class, and suddenly, all the dogs were howling
and testing the extremes of their asphyxiating collars. Roscoe
responded by accelerating away from the danger through my
legs from behind; once clear of my legs, he took an immediate
right turn and changed directions, tangling the leash around
my right ankle and sending me sprawling to the ground backward. The first thing I remember was the smell of a dog's
breath and the immediate sound of growling inches from my
face.

By the end of the third class, I was no longer choking my

dog; he was choking himself by pulling away in random directions to escape. He was now officially more disobedient than when we started. At this point, our esteemed obedience class leader called me aside.

"You are going to need to quit using the collar," he advised. "You have confused the dog by choking him."

"I thought it was called a choke chain collar," I timidly argued; in an attempt to bring some levity, I asked, "Why isn't it called a DON'T choke chain collar?"

"Very funny," he tersely barked.

He said, "Take the collar off and instead, talk to your dog when it is in the right place, and when he wanders off, just stop talking. He wants to hear your voice, so he'll notice the silence and return to your side. "O.K., I'll give that a try..." I said out loud while thinking, "No way that will work."

But it did.

Roscoe was astonished as I reached down and removed the collar, then began petting his head and saying, "Good boy! Good boy!" as I strolled forward. I continued to affirm him, and he walked beside me, looking up for each verbal reward. When he did look around and wander off, I stopped talking, and he would recognize the silence, look back, and return to my side. I was amazed and enlightened. I began to see with my own eyes that obedience is an affirmation exercise, not punishment.

Long after we had returned home and Roscoe was curled up sleeping under the coffee table, I wondered how much of my disobedience could be traced to the fear of cosmic punishment. I had been convinced that breaking the rules would result in a jerk from the divine choke chain to keep me on the straight and narrow path. But like Roscoe's, it didn't work. I was rarely on that path. Instead, I was prone to pull away and choke the life out of myself.

There is no better leash than love.

Chapter Nineteen

19

ON A STICK

"Everything in food is science.
The only subjective part is when you eat it."
- Alton Brown

Remember when the COVID-19 global pandemic delayed and postponed the 2020 Tokyo Olympic Games? Eventually rescheduled, the world's best athletes and performers made their way to Japan, attempting to honor their home countries, vying for the gold, silver, and bronze medals. The games provided a welcome distraction from the ongoing viral threat, while the empty stadium seats served as a reminder that victory and variants coexist.

The Tokyo Games offered rivalry in the traditional Olympic events like track and field, swimming, and gymnastics, as well as new competitions in skateboarding, sports climbing, and surfing. I watched as many competitions as time allowed. I was captivated by two venues, the solo canoe sprint races and rhythmic gymnastics, for both personal and historical reasons.

1. Personal reasons: the 200-meter solo canoe sprint racing champion hails from my hometown. I live in a small town in Washington State, surrounded by the salt water of South Puget Sound. The town's harbor is lined with boats of every kind, from yachts to commercial fishing vessels and sailboats to runabouts. The bay is also home to sport kayaking, stand-up paddle boarding, and solo canoe racing. On any given day, Olympic hopefuls are churning the water, pushing off one knee in the keel of a racing canoe. Living in the training ground for various international competitions creates a personal connection to the sport.

The other event I have a personal affinity with is rhythmic gymnastics. While rhythmic gymnastics is based on dance, it can include different artistic implements, such as hula hoops or batons, but my favorite is the ribbon on a stick. I liked this event because I could never imagine competing in any other Olympic contest. There's no way I can sprint or swim or jump at the Olympic level, but I feel like there's a possibility that I have what it takes for dancing in quasi-Dervish style, twirling the ribbon on a stick. It would still be a stretch, but it seems like my only possible Olympic option. I'm not saying I would medal, but the ribbon on a stick seems like a distant cousin to fly fishing with a soundtrack. Been there, done that.

2. Historical reasons: The gold medal solo canoe sprinter and the gold medal rhythmic gymnast made history as the first women to win the gold medal for their country in each event. Nevin Harrison from the United States won gold in the inaugural women's canoe single 200-meter race. At the same time, Israel's Linoy Ashram became the first Israeli woman to win a gold medal in rhythmic gymnastics.

While both of these competitors are the best of the best at what they do, the way these two competitions are won couldn't be more different. In canoe racing, the athlete lines up at the starting line and stays in a separate lane. The canoe sprinter goes full speed for two hundred meters, lasting about forty-five seconds, within full view of all the boats in the race. The vessels often cross the finish line within a fraction of a second from one another. Slow-motion replay determines the official finish if the race is too close to call in real-time. The first boat to finish wins the gold medal--a very objective process.

Rhythmic gymnastics, however, is an entirely different kind of event. The music drives the performance as the gymnast twirls and spins, trailing the decorative ribbon in concert with the jumps and pirouettes for nearly three minutes. They are not facing their competitors. They are instead facing three sets of judges who evaluate the performance. One group judges the technical value, which includes the difficulty of the composition; the second panel focuses on the artistic value of the routine, and the third group evaluates the performance in terms of execution. The highest total of the judge's scores determines the gold medal winner--a very subjective process.

The difference in competition between objective and subjective results also comes with a difference in response to the win. When American Nevin Harrison was awarded the gold medal for canoe racing, there was no conflict or accusation of an unfair outcome. On the contrary, when Israel's Linoy Ashram was awarded the gold medal for rhythmic gymnastics, there were immediate and ongoing complaints of biased judging and disagreement from her competitors.

This is why some people think the Olympic Games should only include events, like races, that can be objectively decided. There is always room to argue that subjectively judged events, like gymnastics, are awarded based on opinion instead of performance. It is precisely for the subjective outcome that I might have a chance in the ribbon on a stick! It's possible, just maybe, that a judge who appreciates a more full-bodied athlete with a more deliberate artistic interpretation, wielding a unique stick made of driftwood swinging a colorful piece of green ribbon seaweed, that just maybe, I could make some noise in the future of the sport.

But seriously, doesn't this shed some light on our struggles with all things subjective? We want real winners, not winning opinions. One key dynamic when we claim to be correct based on objective facts or what some people call absolutes is the intolerance for the input and opinions of others. In extreme cases, the idea of something absolutely and objectively true eliminates the need to recognize that there are others. Absolutism is the house that legalism builds as we organize our lives according to laws, rules, and regulations. In support of objective outcomes, our language becomes binary: yes or no, black or white, good or bad, right or wrong. Understanding or even admitting complexity can become secondary to the pursuit of certainty. That's why Universities divide academic disciplines into the Arts and Sciences. Science is based on observable and repeatable facts. Data and outcomes drive scientific pursuits. Subjective aspects of interpretation, metaphor, and mystery animate art. How can the two co-exist?

One example can be found in the culinary space. A great deal of science goes into preparing a feast, but it is beyond the scope of the scientific method to experience the smell and taste of a great meal. I lived out this interdisciplinary reality during the Tokyo Olympics! You see, during the entire duration of the 2020 Games, I scientifically and methodically researched and re-built an abandoned Traeger barbecue. Then, on the final day of the Games, I successfully grilled medal-worthy chicken kabobs in honor of the closing ceremonies.

Timeout. Some of you lab coat science types wonder, "Rebuilt the barbecue? You mean you refurbished it, right? I mean, you did not go down to the igniter and the firebox!"

Indeed. I did.

But, you add, "Not the auger motor and convection booster fan."

Believe it. (But believing is so subjective!)

"But surely not the controller with thermostatic feedback and incremental temperature control."

Yes, indeed, porcelain grill bars. You heard it right. I said porcelain.

Stainless steel diffuser plate. Stainless.

After finishing the scientific renovation following objective instructions, I closed the grill cover, fired up the controller to the 'SMOKE' setting, and entered the subjective realm. The sound of that auger depositing pellets to the firebox, the smell of those pecan chips starting to smoke, the rush of the convection fan driving the heat over the stainless diffuser, and wafting through the porcelain grill bars was like the smell and sound of an Olympic stadium, cheering me on as I rhythmically placed the kabobs over the hot grill. The chicken caramelized while the onions and peppers developed their delicious char. The co-existence of the objective and subjective had materialized in my backyard. Science in the technique and art in the taste!

Chicken on a stick for the gold!

Chapter Twenty

20

DON'T KNOW

"Is it ignorance or apathy?
Hey, I don't know and I don't care."
- Jimmy Buffett

I grew up in a remote farming town in the vast rolling hills of Eastern Washington State. The total population of this rural hamlet was less than five hundred people. It meant attending school with the same classmates for twelve straight years. Even with summer and holiday breaks, it was familiarity at a toxic level. I lived out "hyper-local" before it was a thing. I remember feeling a strong "stuck" vibe, as in "this is it" when it comes down to having others to befriend, date, marry, and grow old with. Most locals who went to college in bigger cities or wandered off to "the coast" returned to the farm in due time. In this context, I developed my "what I'm going to do when I grow up" list.

There were the typical entries, like:

- Stay up as late as I want.
- Let my kids eat dessert first.

These kinds of items on my list turned out to be slam dunks.

As it turns out, I do stay up as late as I want; it's just that I don't want to stay up very late at all.

What to eat first is a moot subject since there is no distinction in the nutritional value of desserts over main courses.

Eventually, my list started to include items that proved to be more complex. These were the loftiest goals on my "grow up" agenda:

- Live in another country to experience the world's massive diversity.
- Give my children a gap year break between elementary and secondary education in the twelve-year school cycle. An adolescent sabbatical to rest and make course corrections on the journey to adulthood. Twelve straight years of schooling out of eighteen years of existence seemed excessive.

But, as it turns out, all doable.

An unanticipated employment shift made way for an opportunity to live in the Netherlands for a year. We landed at Schipol Airport in Amsterdam on cold and windy Christmas Day and drove our newly acquired Volkswagen Passat to our row house in a suburb of Leiden. While living in Holland, we toured England, France, Belgium, Germany, Switzerland and Spain.

As a result of our European residence, our children hit the pause button on their academic routines. While taking a hall pass on formal education, the informal and accidental learning during that year abroad was impressive.

We were excited to live and learn, but with our limited Dutch language skills, we had little idea what some of our new neighbors were trying to teach us. Our American sensibilities showed up as clueless confidence, stumbling along wide-eyed, learning new social rules by accidentally breaking them. We lived out the expression, "You don't know what you don't know." The behavior we exhibited as Euro-newbies is documented by a cognitive bias known as the Dunning-Kruger Effect. This behavior is named after the psychologists who studied people like us, who overestimated their capabilities even though they have little or no experience, causing them to overestimate their competence. We often see this behavior in children convinced they could compete at the World Cup level in soccer because they scored two goals in a recent second-grade match on a half-sized pitch. It is ignorance that keeps us from seeing our ignorance. The net result is that we overate ourselves. This cognitive bias is based on unfounded beliefs that we may or may not know we have. Unfounded is a fancier way to say shaky, shady, or both.

Our first experience at the grocery store illustrates our deep-seated Dunning Kruger-ness. After locating our rental row house, we tossed luggage on the beds and headed to the closest grocery store to stock the kitchen. The Dirk van den Broek supermarket in the Shopping Center Winklehof was less than a mile from our new place. Fifty-five years before we arrived in Holland, Dirk, a teenage boy in Amsterdam, began selling milk from a cart that he pushed all around the city. Three years later, Dirk consolidated his mobile milk vending operation to a storefront in the most trafficked public square in Western Amsterdam. From there, he eventually expanded to a chain of more than one hundred and twenty Dirk van den Broek supermarkets. To honor our teenagers, whose lives we had uni-laterally disrupted by relocating them, isolated from lifelong friends, we felt it fitting to get our initial supplies from a former teenage entrepreneur.

When we got to Dirk's parking lot, we drove in circles for ten minutes until a spot opened up. We wondered why it was so crowded. We didn't know. We soon learned that Holland, the most densely populated country in Western Europe, makes waiting an everyday necessity.

We paused at the entry to the store, looking for a shopping cart. There weren't any. We noticed that almost every shopper had a cart, but we began to see how a cart becomes available when someone is done using it and returns it to the cart lock. We watched shoppers return their carts, pushing the front wheels into a locked metal receiver; when the lock clicked, they received a metal coin from the return under the pay slot. We asked one of the returners where we could get a token. She held out her hand and said with an excellent Dutch accent, "It's a gilder, not a token." We didn't know what we didn't know. A gilder is the equivalent of the U.S. dollar. We didn't have a gilder since we hadn't been to a bank to exchange currencies, so I offered the next cart returner a five-dollar bill for his gilder. Dirk would have been impressed with the profit margin.

Having finally solved the cart puzzle, we rolled down the aisle, stacking the cart with groceries. There were cans, jars, shrink-wrapped packages, and containers of all sizes filling up our bright red Dirk van den Broek cart. We pushed our collection to the front of the store, where each line to check out was twelve shoppers deep. Here, in line, we learned that if you leave the slightest space between yourself and the next shopping cart, someone will step in and take that space. They don't say anything; they just cut in and face away. It didn't require a "thank you." It was a literal "Don't mention it." We didn't know what we didn't know.

Once we reached the check stand, we put our grocery items

on the countertop. Immediately, the cashier said, "No, no, no." He motioned to put the items back in the cart and talk to the approaching manager, who pulled the cart aside and instructed us, "You must mark the price on each item before bringing it up to the register." What? He showed us the black grease pencils at the end of each aisle used to write the price on each item. The prices fluctuate so frequently that the store doesn't print it on each item, just on the shelf. We doubled back and made our way around the entire store, trying to find the items we had selected and then writing the prices on each item.

We had officially been shopping for groceries for a couple of hours and began resisting the urge to eat them before purchasing them. We got back in line, careful to close the gap between our cart and the one in front of us, and eventually made it back to the register, where the checker added up our total. Our groceries began to pile up at the end of the checkout counter. "Should we put these in bags?" I asked the checker, who replied, "Did you bring bags?" This is how we discovered that they had no bags. They didn't provide or sell bags. "They are available at the Thursday public market," we were told. Obviously.

We didn't know what we didn't know. So we loaded all the groceries back into the cart, wheeled it out to our car, and dumped everything in the trunk. A friendly young man approached and asked if he could return our cart to the store. How kind! "Bedankt!" I said, trying out my first "thank you" to a local. Halfway home, I realized the nice young man had worked me for a gilder by returning the cart. I was too ignorant to know I was clueless--a classic Dutch case of the Dunning-Kruger Effect.

Here dangles a vital truth: life is an ongoing series of over-confident incompetencies. Most of what we know about how the world works is a direct result of having no idea how the world works. Knowing this means never feeling bad for our clueless confidence! We must continue to plow headlong into getting to know what we don't know. No matter how much somebody knows, at the beginning, they didn't.

It's also "low-hangingly" true that things are more complex than we think.

ACT THREE

ACT THREE

Chapter Twenty-One

BETTER THIS WAY

"Perpetual optimism is a force multiplier."
- Colin Powell

I am an optimist, thanks to my mostly carefree family of origin. My loving parents and happy siblings have contributed to my ability to see the "glass half full."

This doesn't mean I never have bouts of negativity or walk around with a dazed grin. My optimism gets tested. Often.

Over time, I have developed an expression that sums up my outlook: "It's better this way."

I've uttered this short sentence so often that my family and friends have credited me with the phrase, even though the motto is certainly not original to me. A wooden sign displaying this motto hangs over the door in my home office as a reminder to everyone coming and going.

I am willing to admit that "It's better this way" is not always applicable. There are tragic outcomes, like the death of a child or other catastrophic traumas, that exist beyond the scope of this expression. But, outside of those inexplicable losses, this outlook has benefitted me in many ways.

I remember waiting for a flight home after a long week away, only to look at the flight status screen and see the word "CANCELLED." It's at this level of disappointment that my optimistic mantra works so well. Instead of allowing anger or anxiety to take over, I like to push through unexpected difficulties like this by deliberately pondering in what ways it might be better to go on a different flight, meet someone I might have never met, or avoid a catastrophe that I couldn't have anticipated without this interruption. I recognize it as an inconvenience, but re-frame it as a possible inconvenience to my benefit.

This outlook has also served me well in other circumstances. For instance, when a restaurant is out of what I want to order, I see it as an introduction to new smells and tastes I would have never selected. Dis-order can become a discovery. Sometimes, I feel initially disappointed when I want something beyond my means, only to find out later that I don't need it. Whenever plans are interrupted by an unforeseen event, my catchphrase, "It's better this way," can work wonders because it means something beyond what you expected is about to happen. If construction hadn't closed the road, I would never have taken the detour and seen the property where my house now stands for sale. I would never have met my new business partner without that fender bender. Mainly, when something happens that disrupts an agenda, an important lesson emerges.

Most of us have heard others say, "I wouldn't want to go through that again, but I'd never trade it for anything." Aren't they saying that something better emerged through the pain and disruption? That's another version of "It's Better This Way."

In an extreme version of the "better this way" outlook, I have a friend who was diagnosed with final-stage kidney disease that landed him in dialysis for five hours a day, three days a week. I asked him how we would handle it, and he said, "Apparently, somebody at the dialysis clinic needs some encouragement." That's next level I.B.T.W. optimism!

Chapter Twenty-Two

IMAGINE THAT

"Cricket is basically baseball on valium."
- Robin Williams

Baseball has been referred to as the great American pastime. This game, more than any other, provides a comforting, predictable framework of meaning in our unpredictable world. Spring training camps open as the crocus, tulips, and cherry blossoms unfold, and the season extends through the dog days of summer to the end of October. Baseball is baked into the annual rhythm of America's psyche.

But on rare occasions, including player strikes, wars, and pandemics, even baseball has been suspended.

For a vast segment of Americans, suspending baseball makes life seem like an endless winter. Every year, the opening night of baseball season marks the beginning of new possibilities. The reality of canceling baseball's opening night festivities can bring a tear to the eye of any true baseball fan, even a Seattle Mariners fan like me.

On opening night, every team is undefeated, and the flags that fly in center field are not arranged to reflect the team with the most wins, making it possible that the Mariner's flag is not the last one on the edge of right field. The interruption of baseball's historic tradition saddens the heart of any devoted fan, even a Mariners fan like me.

The 1994 suspension of the baseball season created an unlikely moment in Seattle Mariner's history.

I was there, live, in person, when the Mariners won the 7th game of the World Series! You might not remember that.

More specifically, I was in a CBS Radio studio in Seattle in September of 1994 when Hall of Fame broadcaster Dave Niehaus called the imaginary Championship game. "The Voice of the Mariners" had called every Mariners game, from their first game contest against the California Angels on April 6, 1977, to his final game against the Oakland A's on October 3rd, 2010. Thirty-three years, 5,284 games total. His descriptors and catchphrases are a permanent part of Seattle's baseball vocabulary.

"My Oh My!" Niehaus would exclaim when he was overjoyed during the games. "Fly, Fly Away!" was his iconic home run announcement. On the rare occasion that a Mariners player hit a grand slam, Neihaus would burst into his signature call, "Get out the rye bread and mustard, Grandma. It's Grand Salami Time!"

You might not remember or weren't born yet, but in 1994, all professional baseball games were canceled in mid-August due to a player's strike, ending the season and all the playoffs, including the World Series. The Seattle CBS radio broadcast crew decided to capitalize on the missing playoffs by scripting a virtual World Series Championship game with Niehaus calling the game.

The script pitted the Seattle Mariners against the Atlanta Braves in game seven. It was do or die. The audio engineers gathered generic stadium crowd noise but wanted some actual

fans to be in attendance to personalize the broadcast. I was
invited to join the production team, and my job was to cheer in
concert with the game, play by play as if it were happening.

I was sitting in a studio set up with microphones with about
a dozen others, and Dave Niehaus sat through a thick glass
window in an adjacent studio. He had a dozen sharpened
pencils with a scorebook on the desk before him, identifying
the team line-ups. He was leaning into the microphone with his
eyes closed and his reading glasses on his nose at half-mast.
The producer announced in both studios, "Here we go, in 3, 2,
1..."

Dave opened his eyes, looked at us through the glass, and
said, "Live from the Kingdome in Seattle, it's Game 7 of the 1994
World Series..."

He called the entire game in detail. Descriptions of players,
the crowd, the weather, each hit and throw for 27 outs per team.
In the final inning, after the Braves had re-taken the lead, Ken
Griffey Jr. hit a home run, and through the crowd noise, you
could barely hear "Fly Away!"

What a game! I had goosebumps and tears of joy as our
studio erupted with the call of the winning run. It was the most
exciting day in the history of Seattle baseball I'd ever experienced. And it never really happened.

But what did happen again was the global pandemic.
Remember that? We were quarantined and isolated, watching
screens instead of gathering in stadiums, missing the smell of
barbecue smoke from sizzling hot dogs wafting through the air
and the sight of fans leaning into every pitch. We needed help
again. Niehaus was gone, memorialized by a bronze statue
behind home plate in Seattle's stadium. When hope ran out
like a batter with two strikes in the bottom of the ninth, actor
Tom Hanks came through with a hit.

While working on a film project in Australia, he and Rita
Wilson were among the first celebrity couples to go public with

their coronavirus diagnosis. Hanks posted to fans worldwide from down under: "There are things we can all do to get through this by following the advice of experts and taking care of ourselves and each other...Remember, despite all the current events, there is no crying in baseball."

Hanks quoted his character, the manager of an all-female professional baseball team, the Rockford Peaches, from the 1992 Movie A League of Their Own. He encouraged everyone to persevere by remembering that there are things worth crying about, but baseball is not one of them.

He helped remind us that actual loss is not a game, that absolute joy is not imaginary, and that real love cannot be canceled. He helped us see that when we isolate to protect each other, we are part of an effort that dwarfs gathering to cheer each other. Thanks, Tom.

Still. What a game.

Chapter Twenty-Three

DON'T BE A DICKIE

"My fake plants died because
I did not pretend to water them."
- Mitch Hedberg

I discovered it at the bottom of my dresser drawer beneath my seldom used handkerchief collection and nestled in the lost sock pile. I hadn't worn it for decades, probably not since college. I pulled it over my head and looked at myself in the mirror.

Dapper Dickie!

It was my trusty black winter dickie. As soon as I donned it, I felt the sophisticated swagger as it framed my neck with woolen elegance. This vintage 1970s dickie also serves as a neck and upper chest warmer without the bulk of wearing an entire sweater. Right then, I decided it would be the perfect accessory for the birthday celebration on this cold and stormy January night.

By 8 p.m., the party was in full swing when I began to overheat as the roaring fireplace teamed up with a half glass of champagne. Beads of sweat on my upper lip caused me to question the value of my toasty turtleneck add-on. I remedied the swelter by grabbing the upper edge of my nape, hugging undergarment, and simply pulling it off over my head.

Abra Cadabra!

The room went silent before breaking into a roar of laughter when my family saw the turtle neck shirt had no arms or torso, just the neckpiece. That's when I realized my children had never seen one of these portable neck mufflers. The once common faux turtle neck had become a relic. These Millennials and Gen-Xers were very much alive to sleeves of tattoos and all sorts of contemporary fashion accessories; they were dead to the dickie.

Originally named the "detachable bosom," it was more commonly referred to as a "false front" and eventually "dickie" by way of Cockney slang. It was first made of rigid moldable celluloid, think guitar picks and ping pong balls. The dickey allowed office workers in mid-19th century England to look well-heeled without the financial status required to inventory a week's worth of shirts. Eventually, dickies became disposable cardboard accessories for actors in theater productions, eliminating the need to launder critical pieces of wardrobe. The most recent resurrection of the actor's dickie came in 1989 on the big screen with the now classic John Hughes Christmas movie, National Lampoons Christmas Vacation. Actor Randy Quaid, in his best-known role as Cousin Eddie, wore a black dickie under a white sweater during the epic Christmas dinner scene. Even though we've seen that movie almost every holiday season, Eddie's subtle dickie-wear went unnoticed by our children, making my birthday party reveal all the more startling to them.

Why does the dickie garner such disdain? There is, perhaps, a slight sense that others have been fooled when they find out that you are wearing a dickie. At the core of a dickie display lies the intent to deceive. Everyone takes for granted that the advertised neck region is just the visible part of an entire sweater. When you are found wearing only a fraction of a shirt, people wonder what else you might not have. If you are willing to go commando with an accessory, can you be trusted with other wardrobe items? What if the deception creeps into other areas of your accouterment? Does your stylish faux Rolex watch scream that your bank account is at the dickie level? Admit it, isn't the two-year lease on your vehicle just a Tesla dickie? Dickie wearing occasions the question: "What else don't we know about you?" It's common knowledge that faking a turtle neck is often the slippery slope to donning nonprescription glasses.

In addition to the deception, dickie wearing raises a red flag. Specifically the red "sloth" flag. It's evident if you don't have the ambition to put on an entire shirt, chances are that your "most likely to succeed" award from middle school didn't stick. This kind of laziness leads to slip-on shoes and clip-on ties. Dickies justify the "fake it til' you make it" mentality. Dickies are the non-dairy creamers and sugar substitutes of the fashion scene. And in the end, nobody likes a faker.

Remember the infamous financier Bernie Madoff? His asset management firm was advertised as a secure way to invest with exceptional investment returns. After decades of deception, Madoff's accounts turned out to be fraudulent. His wealth management business was a massive Ponzi scheme without any real gains--all fabricated lies. Ultimately, investors lost 65 billion dollars, and Madoff was sentenced to 150 years in prison. Madoff was a notorious investment dickie.

Remember Y2K? Those of us who were alive and partially grown-up were led to believe that on New Year's Day 2000, the beginning of a new millennium, all computers would be rendered useless due to their short-sighted designs, having been programmed with the inability to update. Conspiracy theories circulated dire predictions of food shortages, transportation stand-stills, and disasters. Millions of people stockpiled food and fuel, acquired weapons to protect their stash, and waited for the clock to strike midnight in 1999. When the new millennium arrived...nothing happened. Y2K turned out to be an epic disaster conspiracy dickie.

Dickies continue to abound. There are countless religious dickies preaching doom for donations, not to mention political dickies fabricating promises for potential votes. We continue to see marketing for pharmaceutical dickies, offering addiction as the cure for sickness. We all know what it feels like to get "deeked" by someone posing as authentic.

So, what's the low-hanging lesson? What's the turtle-neck takeaway?

Be the real deal.

Resist the urge to pretend.

Let's not end up style-rich and substance poor.

Keep it real.

Ralph Waldo Emerson summed it up when he wrote: "To be yourself in a world that is constantly trying to make you something else is the greatest accomplishment."

Thanks, Ralph! That's eloquent longhand for "Don't be a dickie."

Chapter Twenty-Four

ALL NIGHT SHOE SHINE

"Black people lived right by the railroad tracks, and the train
would shake their houses at night. I would hear it as a boy,
and I thought: I'm gonna make a song that sounds like that."
- Little Richard

I was twenty years old when I rode a passenger train. It was
a turning point in my life.

I was born into a working-class family. Good people,
salt of the earth. God fearing, whose handshake was as good as
a contract. I was blessed to be counted among them. Still,
nobody in my immediate family had ever graduated from
college. I had aspirations to be the first. I saved what I could in
high school, working summer jobs in the farming economy of
Eastern Washington, determined to pay for the expenses of a
college degree. My savings ran out after my first year, and I
wanted to find a job to cover my tuition and living expenses
moving forward. I found myself living off of government food
stamps, not sure if I could survive, facing the disappointing

option of going back home and ending up as an agrarian laborer.

I had grown up in a strong faith tradition since my dad was the Pastor of our tiny rural church. I remember his frequent lessons on praying and trusting God for provision. I had nodded in agreement to his premise but had never really practiced what he preached. As a starving student, I fell to my knees for the first time and earnestly prayed, "God, if you are real, I need you to show up for me." Deep down, I doubted my situation was something God would notice, considering our world's vastly more urgent needs.

After praying, I headed to the grocery store on Capitol Hill in Seattle to spend the last of my "social and health services" food stamps on dinner. One of the rules for these government-issued food stamps was they could not be used for non-edible goods. This meant that I couldn't buy a newspaper, which, at the time, was the primary source of job postings. I meandered the aisles of the Quality Foods store on eclectic Broadway Avenue, gathering groceries while reading the "want ads" in the classified section of the Seattle Times. I didn't seem to qualify for any of the jobs listed. As I approached the register stand with my collection of goods, I ditched the paper while waiting in the check-out line.

The pair in line before me were chatting, overhearing the one closest to me say to his friend, "I hear they are hiring." I leaned in to get more information, but all I heard was, "Ask for Mr. Morrison." Then, they finished checking out and headed to the parking lot. I realized this could be the answer to my prayer, but at the same time, I wondered if it was just a cruel coincidence. I watched them disappear into the parking lot while paying for groceries. I hurried out the door and saw them standing together, still talking. I walked past them and overheard, "Tell them that your family has a history of working for the railroad; they like to hire people with a railroad history." I walked around the corner, took a pen from my pocket, and wrote "Mr. Morrison/railroad" on the shopping bag. That's all I had, but it was something.

I hurried back home and looked up every railroad I could find. I called the Burlington Northern Santa Fe Railroad and asked for Mr. Morrison. They had never heard of him. I called the Union Pacific Railroad, but they didn't know a Morrison. I dialed the Canadian National Railway, but no luck. I sat back in my chair and began to think I had talked myself into hoping for answered prayer. Just then, I heard a train whistle. I ran to the window and looked out just in time to see an Amtrak train pass. I had been thinking about freight trains the whole time, never considering passenger trains as a possibility. I thought the job might entail working as a brakeman or mechanic, but I have never considered a service job. I dialed the crew base head-quarters for Amtrak in Seattle, and the voice on the other end of the line said, "Amtrak, how may I help you?" I said, "Could I speak to Mr. Morrison?" A short pause, followed by, "One moment, please, while I connect you." I fought back the tears. "Hello. This is Charles Morrison; how can I help you?"

"Um, Mr. Morrison, are you the one to talk to about a job opportunity?"

"I'm the one," he said in a cheerful tone. "Come on down and get an application and an appointment for an interview."

My college roommate gave me a ride to Amtrak's main office, and I grabbed applications for both of us after learning from the clerk at the front desk that Amtrak was looking for over one hundred new hires for a Seattle crew base. I learned all I could about the history of Amtrak. I discovered that after Abraham Lincoln freed the enslaved people in the mid-1800s, a railroad industrialist named George Pullman founded a company in Chicago that manufactured passenger train cars. He hired thousands of newly emancipated Americans as passenger train porters, leveraging their experience to serve others. After decades of forced labor, the chance to wear a uniform and travel across the country attracted the best of the new African American demographic. What initially seemed like an opportunity for the emancipated workers, unfortunately, imposed on them the subservience of former days. The predominantly entitled white passengers expected the porters to treat them so.

Not all porter jobs were the same. Coach car porters oversaw an entire rail car of fifty passengers in seats. Bar and restaurant porters handled the food and beverage service roles. Sleeping car porters were responsible for eleven-bedroom rolling hotels. I filled out a Sleeping Car Porter application. The job entailed serving Amtrak's first-class passengers by stowing luggage, making up the sleeping berths, serving food and drinks from the dining car, shining shoes, and keeping the train cars tidy. They were required to be available night and day to wait on the passengers. For example, the Empire Builder, a passenger train running from Chicago to Seattle, meant being in service for three full days and two nights, one way, then laying over for one night, returning for another three days and two nights. This was a grueling assignment. While the black porters' social standing had been elevated, their working experience resembled the old order. Something had to give.

In 1925, responding to their low wages, long hours, and passenger mistreatment, the Pullman Company's porters formed the Brotherhood of Sleeping Car Porters (BSCP). It was the first all-black labor union in the United States. It was a complex, arduous, and necessary step toward promised equality. The union wielded significant influence on the working conditions and status of the black porters. By the time I got to college, the civil rights legislation that allowed people of color to join all-white unions also created the opening for me to join the formerly all-black Porters union.

When the day for our interviews arrived, my roommate and

I put on our only suit coats, cinched up the knot on colorful ties, donned our best "Sunday" shoes, and headed for Mr. Morrison's office. The lobby was lined with chairs filled with job applicants. Not many wore a suit coat and tie, which made me wonder if we should take them off. Knowing that it's always best to match the look of the interviewer, having never seen Mr. Morrison, we were in a wardrobe quandary. We found a couple of empty seats and waited for someone to call out our name.

My roommate was called first, leaving me nervously waiting alone in a crowded room. I wanted to know if telling Mr. Morrison the truth about my situation was a good idea. We were the youngest in the room, and I doubted he wanted to hire someone who needed a job to finish college. I figured he was looking for a candidate with career aspirations in the travel industry, someone who had always wanted to ride the rails. I planned to work hard, save all I could, and then end my railroad career to finish college and graduate school. I wanted to study moral philosophy and ethics and follow in my father's footsteps as a Pastor. I was caught in a moral dilemma and tempted to lie about my intentions. I wondered if God was testing my mettle, wanting to find out if I had the heart to follow through when the going gets tough. I could hear Dad saying, "I don't care what you are, as long as you're honest." I closed my eyes, took a deep breath, and tried to relax. I opened my eyes while the staffer rounded the corner and said, "Rick Enloe."

I stood up, grinned at the crowd of candidates, turned the corner, and saw my roommate headed toward me. He looked serious, so I couldn't tell how his interview had gone. As we passed each other, our eyes met, and he whispered, "Tell the truth." The door at the end of the passageway opened, and there stood Mr. Morrison. He was wearing a suit and tie. He motioned for me to sit in front of his vast mahogany desk. He glided into his chair opposite me, pulled out my application from a tall stack of papers, took hold of a gold pen as if to take notes, squinting at the paper, and said, "Tell me about yourself."

I shot a gaze to the ceiling behind him, looking for help to find another job after I told the truth and got the "we'll be in touch" response. I dropped my eyes to meet his and said, "Mr. Morrison, I'm in Bible College right now, studying for a future in ministry. I don't have railroad experience, but I think customer service has much in common with ministry."

He put his pen down.

I thought, "Great, here goes."

He stood up and extended his hand toward me. I expected him to say, "I appreciate your time, but..."

Instead, he smiled and said, "Praise God! I've been praying for someone like you. Welcome aboard." It turns out Mr. Morrison grew up in the same church in Colorado that my roommate's family was from. He had been praying that God would send some young men, like Stephen in the Bible, who were full of faith and ready for responsibility. He saw us as answers to those prayers. I had always considered myself a reason to request prayer, never an answer to one.

I joined the Brotherhood of Sleeping Car Porters and began an adventure that has never ended. I learned so much about serving others from the best porters in America. I tended to passengers from Seattle to Chicago and back, providing the means to finish college. My Amtrak days remain a quintessential faith-building, low-hanging moment of truth. Literally.

Chapter Twenty-Five

25

GOING BACKWARD FAST

"You have brains in your head. You have feet in your shoes.
You can steer yourself in any direction you choose. You're
on your own, and you know what you know. And you are the
guy who'll decide where to go."
- Dr. Seuss

Have you ever taken a job that contradicted everything you were preparing for? It seems inevitable that most people over their working years would be able to describe at least one job that they found ill-fitting and eventually intolerable. It's the point in your career journey when you realize you're going backward.

My employment anomaly came right after graduating from college. I took the job out of desperation, hoping to survive financially and unsure of other options. It wasn't remotely in the same universe as I had been schooled to do. I had studied literature and philosophy, hoping to find a role as a teacher. Instead, I found myself driving a forklift and greasing zerks on a colossal machine that rotated stainless steel molds filled with plastic resin that would eventually become chemical containers. The work was dirty, exhausting, and demanding. One of the worst parts for me was how early in the day the job started. I was a production team member, so my factory shift started at five a.m. daily. To show up by five a.m., I had to wake up at four a.m., dress quickly, and head out the door by four twenty. I'd drive my beat-up, pewter grey Chevy stations wagon half a block down the street from my apartment to the corner mini-mart and grab some breakfast. I ignored the parking stripes in front of the mart since there were no other cars on the road; cranking the steering wheel hard right, I'd jump the short curb and pull in, past the gas pumps, and park parallel to the front door. Hopping out of the car, I'd leave the engine running to warm it up, then jog in and fill a jumbo cup of self-serve coffee, grab a maple bar by the check stand, and toss a $5 bill on the counter for the $4.50 coffee donut combo and head back to the car.

I was the undisputed first customer of the day, day after day, for the better part of a year. Three hundred empty coffee cups in the backseat testified to the efficiency of my morning routine.

Then, one morning, I pulled up to the mini-mart, past the gas pumps, and parallel to the door. I slumped out of the car, rubbed my eyes, left the driver's side door ajar, and went through the motions to start my morning. After tossing the $5 on the counter, I returned to the front door with my coffee and pastry in hand and immediately realized that my car, always visible from inside the store, was gone.

"Oh man," I blurted out, startling the clerk, "Somebody stole my car!" I instantly regretted leaving the car running and the driver's side door open. I walked slowly toward the door, wondering who I could call at this early hour to get a ride to work. As I approached the driver's side door, I was startled by the sight of my car going backward in the street with the door flapped open and nobody in the driver's seat. In my haphazard approach to parking, I hadn't secured the column shifter securely in park, so it had dropped back into reverse and was now the world's first self-driving station wagon. The steering wheel was turned to starboard, so it did a giant backward circle, jumping up the curb, barely missing the gas pumps, then jumping back down the curb and onto the empty street. All in reverse. Since I had just started the car, the engine was revving with the choke engaged, allowing the vehicle to pick up speed with each lap.

I dropped my coffee and pastry and ran into the street, attempting to gain access to the driver's seat. Since the car was going backward, I got in position and jumped onto the open door, feet dragging on the pavement, grabbing the steering wheel, and pulling myself into the seat. I grabbed the gear shift and threw it into the park, causing an abrupt screeching sound as the car stopped, followed by a sharp pain as I slammed my forehead into the dashboard. I flopped back into the seat, looked into the rearview mirror, and saw that the car's rear bumper was six inches from the gas pumps. I had narrowly avoided a 4:45 a.m. 911 call and a probable fiery explosion.

I carefully put the car in drive, appropriately parked, shut off the engine, cleaned up the spilled coffee and dented maple pastry, got back into my car, and just sat there staring out the front window at the empty street in the dark. I felt tears welling up in my eyes and said out loud, "What am I doing?" At that moment, I realized this near disaster was a metaphor for my current life.

Can you relate? Ever felt like you have haphazardly parked yourself in a situation only to realize everything in your life was going backward fast, out of control with no direction, and bound to implode? That's how I felt. My grandfather gave me financial advice once. He said, "If you can't keep up, you won't catch up." Finding direction in my life or catching up to my purpose seemed impossible when I was going the wrong way.

Then, as I put my car in drive and started slowly down the street, the low-hanging truth hit me: It's not about the vehicle; it's a driver issue. I blamed my aimlessness on my job, but jobs are vehicles that need driving. I had become an observer of my life from the curb instead of the pilot of my purpose. It was early in the morning on that day that I took new responsibility for where I was headed, and it's been quite a ride.

Chapter Twenty-Six

PARTY PLANNER

"There are basically two types of people. People who accomplish things, and people who claim to have accomplished things. The first group is less crowded."
- Mark Twain

This writing outlines my Types of Humanity Theory. I build my hypothesis on years of human interaction, concluding that there are two types of people in the world: Party People and Planning People. Party People are famously afraid that they might miss out on some fun. "FOMO" animates them. Meanwhile, Planning People are worried they will be unprepared for unseen eventualities. They have the "What-Ifs."

Party people spend their young lives at the expense of their end-of-life well-being. Eventually, they will discover it's called a liver because you need it to live. Pure planners are delayed gratification gurus, willing to slog through the best years of life, saving instead of spending, to dominate in the senior zone.

They fly high with pensions that fuel their daily water aerobics, four-seater golf carts, and tile-rummy marathons. They know how to stay out of the kitchen in pickleball because they stayed out of the kitchen in mid-life. It is the opposite for team Party, who know a béchamel from a mirepoix and have the cholesterol numbers to prove it. They weren't interested in climbing the corporate ladder and eventually would lose interest in climbing stairs.

I am more of a party person than a planner. I mean, I thought they called it "disposable income" because you were supposed to dispose of it. My Party Spouse and I collaborated on producing two other human beings who referred to me as "Dad." My concern about their financial future led me to read the book Rich Dad/Poor Dad. I read through chapters titled: "The Rich Don't Work for Money" and "The Rich Invent Money." I didn't recognize any of the rich Dad behaviors describing my parenting. I learned that since a poor Dad had mentored me, I would pass the legacy of scarcity to my children. I admitted this to my two sons in an official apology when they were in high school.

"Guys," I shared over the breakfast table one Saturday between bites of pigs in a blanket, "After reading the book Rich Dad/Poor Dad, I'm sorry that I didn't know how to be a rich dad instead of a poor dad. Forgive me."

They allowed me a moment of silence before editing my apology. My youngest son said, "Dad, those are not the only choices. What about Happy Dad/Sad Dad? A lot of my friends have rich dads who are sad and mean." He wasn't ruling out happiness AND prosperity, but expressing a sensibility that there is a difference between wealth and well-being. Our less-than-affluent status had not blinded him from the joy that undergirds everything. I love that!

Then, my eldest son, a true poet, artistically summed it up by saying, "Maybe we should stop asking ourselves if others see us as rich or poor and think about whether we are helpful or helpless?" In this expression, he summed up the party and planner equation. When we plan to be helpful, we discover true festive. It is in giving that we receive.

In one short sentence, which most often poets alone can see, he expressed a unified theory that encompasses both party and planner in one. It was not an "either-or" way to think but a "both-and" way to see things.

How many other bifurcations could be expanded and re-imagined by stepping back and considering a third way? Privilege need not cancel compassion. Wealth can include well-being. But only if we don't allow labels to distract us from lesser-known low-hanging truths.

.

Chapter Twenty-Seven

WHAT YOU DO

"It isn't what you do, but how you do it."
- John Wooden

I am a member of the men's club at our local public golf course. A classic "munie." I look forward to the club's collection of monthly tournaments. Each tournament has a different format. There's the three clubs and a putter tournament where, as it sounds, only four clubs are allowed. Players can pick any three clubs and a putter. This event teaches you how carrying a full bag doesn't change the outcome much. Alternate shot contests, two and four-person competitions, and individual medalist play exist.

Most of the men in the club are retired, and their best scoring days are behind them, making tournament scoring bogie-intensive. The tournament payouts include flights for gross and net scores, incentivizing even the high handicappers.

While I may not see many great shots, the banter between players and the endless reel of recycled jokes is impressive.

On my way to the course, I hit the accelerator and changed lanes to expedite my arrival to my favorite tournament of the year, the two-person best ball. It's a genuine team competition, where two players hit the ball, then choose the best shot and hit again. It's a chance to make new friends and disappoint them. I arrived with enough time to spare to hit a few warm-up shots on the driving range. After hitting a few balls into the adjacent forest, I noticed the club pro heading in my direction, waving at me.

"Meet Benny-he's your best ball partner for today's tournament," he hollered, pointing to the guy standing beside me with a yellow hat and matching sweater.

"Hi," he said, leaning in and reaching for a handshake.

"Nice to meet you, Benny. I'm Rickey," I replied while shaking hands with vigor.

We both hit two more duck hooks, grabbed our clubs, and headed back to the carts lined up for the start.

"So, what do you do for a living?" Benny bluntly quizzed me.

This is a common question when meeting someone new. I understand why we would ask it. When we know what somebody does, we build ideas about what they are like. Even so, I've always enjoyed giving an indirect answer to the question of "What do you do?" to avoid the silent, awkward moment if I answered candidly, "I care for people who are facing their greatest challenges and trying to decipher life's most profound questions."

I look him in the eye, push back on the bill of my vintage Scottish red beret, and reply, "Technically, my work happens at the intersection of moral philosophy and practical theology. How about you?" His eyes rolled back, and he laughed, "I'm retired, so I work at the intersection of napping and gardening."

We laughed, moved onto the first tee, and promptly hit our opening drives into the shallow pond. We drove out the approximate location of our lost balls, dropped shiny new orbs onto the dewy grass, and waited to hit until the group cleared the green.

Looking down the fairway, Benny said, "Seriously, what do you do for a living?"

I said, "O.K. We could all use a tour guide through life's most difficult journeys, right? I signed up to walk with people in times like that. Kinda like a sherpa who helps carry the luggage on a mountain climb."

"This is like being on a game show!" Benny laughed, "I'm never gonna get a straight answer from you."

I call this the "identity quandary." We all spend a great deal of time trying to figure out what makes others tick, but the quest is never quite over. We do the same thing with ourselves.

With so many philosophical and theological answers to what we do, it can be complex, and sorting out which intersection to build our identity on is challenging. We all need to decide for ourselves. Others will certainly make recommendations for us, and some explanations sound like sales pitches, hoping that those inquiring will buy our version of ourselves. Ultimately, each of us learns how to express our purpose guided by a moral and spiritual compass.

In her book The Power of Ethics, author Susan Liautaud writes about the danger of living in a culture that has compromised truth. "The epidemic of 'alternative facts' or what I call 'compromised truth' is one of our time's most insidious and dangerous global systemic risks. Compromised truth is the single greatest threat to humanity. It topples our ability to make ethical decisions."

What we are looking for is actual versus alternative truth. Fortunately, truth is all around us and running into us when we take the time to step back with curious introspection and consider the narratives of our everyday lives. Life lessons, framed by our daily experiences, are like one of those magic eye posters; we must stop, stare, slow down, and contemplate to see. Even our humiliating experiences can teach us true humility, while our willingness to experience risk can offer the low-hanging truth about rewards that cannot be accessed otherwise.

I'm hoping to encourage the emerging philosopher and theologian in all of us. Everyone thinks, but philosophers think again. Everyone asks for help, but the theologian asks God for help.

Often, when something is identified as low-hanging fruit, it is a label for things on the peripheral. Things that are inconsequential to the paramount endeavor. Something that takes little effort. In a business context, when someone says, "The real profit is not in the low-hanging fruit," it means low-hanging is not essential. Too shallow.

But for me, and maybe you too, low hanging-in can also refer to discovering insights that are easily accessible, like a sidewalk with a ramp. Reachable. Inclusive. In common. Through this lens, life can include micro sketches of truth available and accessible to the wide-eyed and open-eared.

Like railroad tracks, we need an appreciation for wisdom (philosophy) and transcendent advice (theology) to keep our lives moving in the right direction and eventually arrive at our destination.

Chapter Twenty-Eight

SINCERELY WRONG

"Back of every mistaken venture and defeat
is the laughter of wisdom if you listen."
- Carl Sandburg

Seattle's rainstorms often express themselves in the early morning. However, now and again, by late afternoon, a welcome flash of sunshine can break through the clouds. This inconsistency in the region's weather pattern can cause commuters to forget to grab umbrellas on their return trip home, leading to the gradual stockpiling of umbrellas at the office.

Such was the case with Bill. He'd carry an umbrella out of the house early each work day, use it while waiting for the morning bus, and then toss it behind his desk at the office. On the occasional sunny afternoon, Bill would head to the bus for the evening commute and forget to bring the umbrella home. Throughout the winter, he methodically and haphazardly created a serious umbrella overstock at the office.

As the umbrella pile at work grew, Bill would mentally rehearse the return of the entire umbrella family to its place at home. Yet, every sunny afternoon, he would unwittingly and regrettably forget to bring the umbrellas home. Something about the rush to catch the bus home gave the behavior its routine. He quickly glanced around to make sure his phone was on the charger, the frantic paper shuffling as the clock ticked down the arrival of the afternoon bus. Most of all, the bright glare of sunshine reflected off the adjacent buildings subconsciously but powerfully, permitting him to leave without umbrella protection.

For the seasoned Northwesterner, each new stormy morning brought the frantic search for an umbrella. Most true Northwest homes have a decent collection of bumbershoots. Most were purchased in the panic of a downpour if it happens in a retail establishment where umbrellas are sold. Many were birthday or Christmas gifts or, perhaps, a free incentive included in the purchase of cologne or the subscription to a magazine.

By the time all the standard umbrellas had been put into service and abandoned at the office, the spring rains would give rise to the household's final available rain shields, namely, the golf umbrella. They are the circus tent of the umbrella family. While acting as the last line of defense against the downpour, they did, at the same time, prove to be the friendliest of all umbrellas since they protected not only the carrier but the adjacent ten to twelve bystanders. Brightly colored and magnificent in scope, they signify that a guy is down to his last umbrella.

Then it happened. The harsh and stormy morning when an umbrella is desperately needed, but every domestic unit has a business address. Standing by the bus holding a newspaper over his head, starting the commute half-soaked, Bill finds a seat on the bus and reads the soggy editorials all the way to his umbrella-laden office. As the bus pulled up to the office out of habit, Bill grabbed the umbrella beside him and started off the bus. The umbrella's owner- a fiery woman in a red coat- grabs it and says, "Hey, that's my umbrella; give it back!"

"I'm so sorry--my mistake!" Bill mumbles as he hands the umbrella back .

The embarrassment of the morning's misunderstanding reminded Bill to restock and bring his entire office collection back home. So, when quitting time rolled around, he collected the small umbrellas, the cane-handled plaid beauty, the concise blue and black travel umbrellas, and the giant golf dome.

With his briefcase in one hand and a dozen assorted umbrellas under the other arm, he jumps onto the steps of the afternoon bus and locks eyes with the woman in the red coat from the morning bus.

The disgust on her face fueled a loud response, "You've had a good day, haven't you?" She wheeled around and announced to the commuters, "Watch your umbrellas! This guy rides around all day and steals umbrellas. He tried to pick mine this morning!" The woman, playing judge and jury, had figured out what was up based on her personal experience and observation: this guy steals umbrellas.

Makes sense.

But not true.

She was sincere but sincerely wrong. She was mad but mistaken. What she thought was happening was not happening. Bill was simply taking his collection of personal umbrellas home.

This begs the question: what if your observations lead to reasonable but untrue explanations? How often have you wondered if you were wrong when convinced you were right?

Here's some low-hanging truth: conclusions based solely on our own experience and observations are seldom accurate. In most cases, questions work better than loud conclusions in our search for what is really going on.

Chapter Twenty-Nine

BISCUIT BLAST

"So the pie isn't perfect? Cut it into wedges.
Stay in control, and never panic."
- Martha Stewart

I t was a hot day, even by Arizona standards, when Sam pulled into the Scottsdale Fiesta Shopping Center to pick up some groceries for the weekend. He maneuvered into a parking spot right next to a car with a woman sitting in the driver's seat. Sam glanced into the car on the way to the store's entrance and noticed her eyes closed as if napping, but her right hand held her head. Strange, but none of his business, he figured. About ten minutes later, after grabbing a few items, Sam strolled out of the store and saw the same woman in the same position, with her hand behind her head, but now her eyes were wide open with a look of panic.

Sam approached the car and gently opened the door. The woman maintained her position, frozen in place, looking forward with her hand holding tightly onto the back of her head.

"Is everything alright?" he asked.

"No!" she exclaimed. "I've been shot in the head, and I can feel my brain!"

"Oh, my God!" Sam muttered as he stepped back, dropped his groceries, and frantically dialed 911 for help.

The paramedics, dispatched from Scottsdale Fire Department Station Two, roared into the grocery store's parking lot only minutes after the emergency call. They learned from Sam that the woman's name was Maria; she was 68 years old and lived in a rough part of town, just a few minutes from the Fiesta Shopping Center.

The lead paramedic jumped to the driver's side of the car and tried to convince the woman to take her hand away from her head. She would not. She was convinced that her hand was keeping her brain in her skull. Finally, as the paramedic pried her hand away, he began to laugh, and he didn't stop until he couldn't breathe.

As soon as he caught enough air to form a sentence, he yelled, "Ma'am, you haven't been shot, and you are not holding your brains in!"

Maria had arrived at the shopping center an hour earlier. She made her weekly rounds, checking off each item on her list: milk, eggs, coffee, biscuits, and dog food. She paid for her groceries, returned to her car, and placed the bag of groceries in the back seat of her car. The interior of her vehicle was sweltering due to the summer sunshine, with all the windows closed. She placed the shopping bag in the back seat on the driver's side of the car; by chance, the refrigerated biscuits (packaged in the cardboard tube with metal ends) were sticking out of the bag, pointing directly at the back of the driver's seat.

In the amount of time, it took to open the driver's side door, locate her keys, start the car, and buckle her seatbelt--the tube of biscuits had expanded in the heat of the car's interior, sending the metal end of the biscuit tube flying toward the back of her head with a loud 'pop.' The metal end also had one biscuit attached to it!

Maria heard the popping sound, and since she lived in a neighborhood where drive-by shootings were common, she figured it sounded like a gunshot. She had always feared that someday a stray bullet could end her life like she'd seen so often on the news. She immediately felt a pain in the back of her head as the metal cap hit her, and she reached back with her left hand and felt a cool, sticky, gooey, pasty substance. In her panic, she concluded that she had been shot and she was holding her gray matter from escaping her skull.

The paramedic repeated, "Ma'am, you need to relax! You are holding a biscuit to your head!" But Maria could not relax. She had spent 20 minutes believing her life was over. Her heartbeat was dangerously elevated, and her body had gone into shock. She had processed regrets, retrieved her best memories, and started grieving her loss. Although she ultimately survived this 'pseudo shooting,' she needed medical attention until she was stable enough to return home. All because she had been holding a biscuit to her head. It took Maria a couple of weeks to finally crack a smile and start to tell the story of her mistaken demise.

If we stop and think for a minute, aren't we all susceptible to mistaking what's happening at some point? Don't we all draw conclusions based on our fears and deepest concerns? At best, they are called assumptions or, at worst, conspiracy theories. We all seem poised to confirm our own biases. Our assumptions are often more potent than the accurate instruction of others.

If we look back on our lives, how many times have we panicked, thinking our futures and relationships were undone by jumping to conclusions, only to find out that we were holding a biscuit to our heads? In a frightening world, hysteria seems like the default low-hanging option, creating the worst-case scenario out of a perfectly reasonable situation.

An outside observer uncovered the truth here. That is a profound low-hanging takeaway. We all need a biscuit inspector. Someone willing to come running when we are at wit's end. Who is that for you? Who are you for others? Also, making biscuits from scratch is better than buying tube ones. Just sayin'.

Chapter Thirty

30

LOOKING DOWN

"The risk of love is loss, and the price of loss
is grief. But the pain of grief is only a shadow when
compared with the pain of never risking love."
- Hillary Stanton Zunin

The third diagnosis of her young life announced cancer's return for the final time. Having stared down the dread maladie for five years, since seventh grade, her college years would be her last.

It is most fitting that she crossed over in April, timing her passage with the blooming Paperwhites pushing through the rain-soaked soil of the Pacific Northwest and the church bells waking from the silence of Maundy Thursday. It was resurrection season, and she participated most tangibly.

Hundreds gathered at the chapel on the hill to remember and celebrate her abbreviated life. Her father's tribute pierced my core. It was this same father that God had called me to care for.

I'd visited the hospital in her waning stages. The room was filled with the strange duet of slow breathing and the infusion pump's intermittent harmony as she rested in solemn silence. Even so, leukemia could not mute a fiercely held faith in her Creator's love, following a path cleared by her parent's example.

Weeks earlier, when the total weight of dread descended on her family, I wondered what, if anything, I could do to stand with her father under the burden of the impending loss. I did not want to intrude on this tragic and holy space. It seemed that the expressions of care often could unintendingly trivialize this complexity of grief beyond imagination.

Considering how I might help, I sat silently, staring out a window facing the emerald waters on the starboard side of my home. I suddenly remembered what my Dad had whispered to me while attending my Grandmother's funeral at age twelve. "Loss can lower a person's gaze," he whispered, "Most times causing them to look down at a time like this. It's not a bad idea to shine their shoes if you can; that way, through the tears, they can be reminded that somebody cares." It seemed consistent with Jesus washing his friend's feet the night before they lost him.

That became my plan. Shine his shoes before a memorial service commenced. I called a close friend of the father and asked him if he could somehow collect his dress shoes. The ones most likely to be worn to the funeral. He was able to creatively gather six pairs that he considered to be memorial service candidates.

The fact is, I knew how to shine shoes, working my way through college as a porter on overnight passenger trains from Seattle to Chicago. The trains offered free shoe shines to each first-class passenger. I learned how to clean, polish, buff, and detail every kind of shoe imaginable. I spent several hours applying all my shoe-shining acumen to these six pairs.

When the shoes were ready, I drove to this father's house at night, parking a block away to stay unnoticed, carrying the six pairs of immaculately shined dress shoes in a large paper shopping bag. I crept up to the porch, carefully placing the bag adjacent to the front door. As I turned to sneak away, the door opened, and the man who owned these shoes said, "What are you doing here?"

I turned around, met his gaze, and said, "I shined your shoes."

Silence.

"I mean, I didn't know what else to do, so I shined your shoes so you would know that I care and you're not alone in this."

His stern and concerned demeanor melted into a smile. He opened the door and said, "Please, come in."

Shiny shoes for a memorial service began a journey of tears, hugs, and abiding friendship.

What's the prevailing low-hanging takeaway? Love never fails--even the slightest and most feeble expression of care multiplies. When your head is stuck, follow your heart. Faith buoys us, hope steadies us, and love invites us in.

Chapter Thirty-One

ADVICE FOR THOSE I LOVE

"Good advice is always certain to be ignored,
but that's no reason not to give it."
- Agatha Christie

H ave you ever seen or used those "conversation
starter" cards? There are all sorts of them for various
occasions and settings. Some cards are designed as
"ice-breakers," posing questions to get people talking. Others
are for special events or specific age groups. Recently, I
attended a holiday dinner for board members of a local non-
profit. Our host placed cards at each table, and during the
break between the main meal and dessert, we went around the
table and answered the questions individually. It was only after
the first guest turned over her card with a puzzled look on her
face that our host realized the "Ice Breaker" questions were
from an "Adult" conversation starter box." The well-dressed,
recently retired first-time guest of this holiday gathering looked
at her card and said, "Is this serious? Why is it anybody's business what turns me on?"

Her question met with gasps, stifled laughing, and the sight of coffee coming out of her husband's nose.

Apologies were accepted, and we moved on with a new and more civilized set of question cards. When my turn came, I flipped the card to reveal, "What advice would you give to those you love?" I thought briefly and offered, "When you come to a fork in the road, look around for the spoon and knife, and you'll have a complete setting." I didn't have much time to think about it. We chuckled and moved on, even though most people were still thinking about what turned them on.

Since that holiday dinner, I have reflected on this question. It's a good question. So, here's my more thoughtful two-fold advice to those I love: Know how to keep your head up and keep moving forward. Shorthand version: Chin up and gear up. Are you already picturing a CUGU tattoo?

I am compelled to advise this, knowing that real life comes with moments that strip us of every motivation besides the sheer power of will. Sometimes, it can be self-inflicted; when you over-book and over-commit "while vowing never to do it again", you gave your word to others who are counting on you, so keep your head up and power through. One foot in front of the other.

Sometimes, it is not self-inflicted, like when you host an uninvited viral malady. You had plans, and being sick wasn't one of them. But now you feel unwell. Whether you have tested positive for something that requires isolation or have something nobody else wants, it becomes clear that plans must be shuffled. When those plans were something you looked forward to, disappointment can overshadow the illness, and chins can lose altitude. It's at times like these that we need chin lifters. People who understand and want to make a meal, mow the lawn, pick up the kids, take the dog for a walk, and sit with you in the tough times. We all need them and have what it takes to be them.

When I'm overwhelmed, I like to imagine my next chance to re-group. When I can find space and solace, I'll say, "Chin up! Before long, you'll get through this, and you won't believe what's next."

We've all heard, "Find out what you are passionate about doing and make it your life's work," as if there is a dream occupation that is a constant "chin-upper." Truthfully, jobs seldom feed passion, but they can often fund them. I've vaccinated dairy cows, scrubbed the mineral ring off public school toilets, changed sprinkler pipes on a steep hillside in the dark, and taught countless classes to students who attended to get the credits instead of fueling their curiosity. I've waited through the night in hospice for the inevitable, stood in silence at the scene of a profound loss, and sat with people so torn in grief that they could not stop weeping.

All chin-downers for me.

Chin downers are life's turnovers, but progress means ensuring more assists than turnovers.

It's fair to say I've experienced way more sweetness and grace than dismal, passionless endeavors.

I hope we all recall times when we said, maybe even out loud, "I wish this could never end."

Walking on the beach hand in hand with the only person who really knows you and still loves you.

Reading Magdalena Catalina at bedtime to an audience of laughing littles.

Teaching to people who are eager to learn and grateful for the lesson.

Taking random ingredients from the refrigerator and curating a delicious meal to serve to others.

Cruising through Liverpool in a hippie van in a tie-dyed shirt, singing Beatles songs where they were first performed.

Hoisting a Chinook Salmon over the transom of a Boston Whaler in South Puget Sound.

Pouring Dungeness crabs fresh from the pots onto a picnic table covered in butcher paper with Old Bay seasoning wafting over lifelong friends, watching them eat and laugh until they'd had their fill.

But honestly, the only way to get to the treasured moments is to keep your chin up and advance.

So, when you are so lonely, your heart hurts, waiting for the delayed flight home, and it gets canceled. Keep your chin up.

When you have to do something again that you've done a hundred times, and it seems like it will never end, do it again.

And even if you get diagnosed with stage four cancer and all your plans go opaque, keep your chin up, put one foot in front of the other, and keep thinking, "Chin up! Before long, you'll get through this, and you won't believe what's next."

ALSO BY RICK ENLOE

Go to www.lowhangingtruth.com for a chance to win Low-Hanging Truth giveaways and to leave helpful or cheerful comments for Rick. This site has a grouch filter, so it's not a good place for carping, grousing, or general malcontent.

Here's an excerpt from Rick's Upcoming Novel:
Every Grace That Brings You Near

Death is always big news in a small town like St. Jimmy.

I've lived here all my life and can only remember a handful of times when an ambulance from the city roared down the main street, sirens screaming, announcing our very own emergency.

In each case, it was bad news for somebody, and this time was no different.

It was ten o'clock on a summer Sunday morning, the sun

spilling over the horizon and peeking through the rolling hills of Washington State's Whitman County. The morning sun illuminated three-story high-grain elevators just behind Main Street. A quarter mile down the road, golfers were making the turn on the six-hole golf course at the edge of town. The city council decided it would be better to have a well-maintained six-hole course than a nine-hole course with ratty greens. They also uniquely decreed that the green fees should be paid when you are finished golfing, not before you teed off. They figured you might not know how many holes you would play until after the fact, and mostly, it allowed the losing golfers to pay for the winner's round. The Sunday morning tee times were in direct competition with the church services in town.

Many churchgoers played golf, but not on a Sunday morning. Chief among the Sabbath keepers were the Pentecostals. While Top Flight balls landed in the pond on the par three fourth hole at the Country Club, Pastor Mickey read Acts chapter five to the twenty-two Pentecostal worshippers at the Church of What's Next, just two blocks east of Main Street. He was reminding the faithful in attendance of the story of Ananias and Saphira, the couple who were struck dead by the Holy Spirit for lying. Mickey paused and solemnly delivered the final verse in the reading: "Great fear seized the whole church and all who heard about these events." He closed the Bible with a dramatic thud just as the ambulance from the city rounded the corner past the golf course, red and blue lights flashing in time with its howling siren, straight past the church, then down the main street and across the railroad tracks and out of town. A holy hush fell over the congregants when they heard the sirens, "Every eye closed, and every head bowed," Pastor Mickey said in a somber tone.

A chorus of neighborhood dogs started howling in unison, their owners looking out windows and front porches, expecting the rescue vehicle to move fast.

But it wasn't. The ambulance was traveling the speed limit, causing everyone to figure its mission was more retrieval than resuscitation.

Details of the emergency traveled faster than the vehicle. In St. Jimmy, the first responders were the holy helper's prayer partners. If you wanted to know details of breaking news in town, you heard it through the grapevine after you heard it through the prayer line.

The original call for help came to the St. Jimmy telephone company switchboard through a party line, interrupting Carl Peterson and his new girlfriend Lila from Pine City, discussing their Sunday night square dancing plans at the Grange Hall. Marie, the St. Jimmy telephone switchboard operator for the past forty years, startled by multiple calls on a Sunday morning, forgot to unplug the Petersons when she pushed the phone wire into the switchboard to connect to the call. A panicked and slightly muffled female voice on the line said, "Come quick, I'm at the Cleetus Ranch, and Bobby ain't breathin'!"

Carl and Lila heard the woman's desperate cry for help. Carl interrupted, "Marie, I'll go for help!" He dropped the phone and ran out of his house, down the porch stairs, and across the barnyard to his pickup truck. He threw open the door of the old three-quarter ton International Harvester, unholstered the CB radio, depressed the side button on the microphone, and blurted, "Mayday, Mayday, Mayday," to alert the volunteer fire department of the unfolding emergency. Carl- having skipped cardio workouts for the past decade, started huffing and puffing the news of Bobby's demise on the radio while cranking up the old rig. He realized nobody on channel 16 could tell what he was trying to say, so he raced toWart the main street, spewing diesel smoke from the rusty trap wagon, skidding into the fire station driveway. He jumped out and pulled the siren switch on the emergency box attached to the corner of the building. Meanwhile, Lila had already called the Holy Helpers Prayer line, putting in an urgent request for Bobby Cleetus and his unconscious condition, setting the gossip network into a phone calling frenzy that Marie could hardly manage at the telephone switchboard.

Like other farming towns, a daily tradition in St. Jimmy was the "noon whistle." The fire station siren was automatically set to go off every day at high noon, alerting the town folks that it was time for lunch. But everybody knew something was seriously wrong if it ever went off before or after noon. As the piercing siren echoed off the grain elevators at ten o'clock, the volunteer fire department team approached the station from the surrounding neighborhood. St. Jimmy's finest were headed down the street in golf carts, bicycles, and on foot. Volunteer Fire Chief Nappie Webb was the last to arrive, managing the two blocks from the Red and White grocery while finishing a powdered sugar donut. Just as Nappie darkened the door, the red phone at the station rang. He unholstered the phone. Marie was on the line; she choked back her tears and blurted out, "Old man Cleetus is dead!"

The card tables at the back of the Rialto Tavern were packed that night. Conversations swirled around the unfolding details of the day. The ugly truth was that Old Man Cleetus had entertained his mistress at the ranch while his wife was at church. Mrs. Cleetus 'got religion' at the Spring revival services a few years back and had since started faithfully attending the Sunday services at the Church of What's Next. Everybody in town knew the Pentecostals' worship service lasted at least three hours each Sunday morning, which was ample time to do a little entertaining back at the Cleetus homestead. The old man's final romantic encounter ended abruptly when he'd doubled the Viagra dose, and his ticker gave way.

Rumors had been circulating the Red and White Grocery coffee table that the cleaning lady from the Wagon Wheel Motel in Steptoe had been making the fourteen-mile drive for a few months. Prayer line details revealed she'd been showing up with fresh lipstick and no scrub bucket, indicating that cleaning was not on the list of reasons for a Sunday morning visit.

As the story developed around the tables at the Rialto, one of the prayer warriors shared a juicy detail that had everybody leaning in and looking up. "So and so overheard Mrs. Cleetus talking while getting a perm at the Chat N' Curl. She said, "In confidence, I suspect something was going on with Bobby, so I asked Pastor Mickey to talk some sense into him." Nappie took a long draw from his pint, wiped his mouth with his sleeve, and added, "I heard Pastor Mickey paid the old man a visit at the ranch, and they had some words! Bobby told him it was none of his business how he lived his life. I guess Pastor Mick told him that he wasn't the one to worry about, that God was in charge, and if he decided to stand between God and his wife, the Holy Spirit would come calling."

Wart, the bartender general manager of Rialto, reached over Nappie's shoulder to refresh his Coors light and said abruptly, "Still, nobody ever imagined it would end up with her standing in the front yard, wrapped in a bedspread while they carted the old man out with a white sheet pulled over his face.

And a great fear fell over all who had heard these things.

ABOUT THE AUTHOR

The Enloe family house sits across the street from the salt waters of South Puget Sound on the Island of the Foxes in Washington State. Rick is Marvelea's husband and Dad to Matt, Nicole, Grant, and Tiffany. He is also Grampy to Kai, Scotland, Blu, Pax, and Goldie. Rick teaches moral ethics, grounded in sacred ancient Middle Eastern texts, on the weekends. Beyond teaching and writing, Rick enjoys producing podcasts, losing golf balls, and making art in his closet-sized man cave in the forest.

Other little known details about Rick...

- He played professional football for four hours
- He got lost snow skiing in Switzerland and ended up in Italy.
- He successfully gave CPR to a man who was choking on meatloaf.
- He won a Ping-Pong tournament using his shoe as a paddle.
- He is an accomplished amateur chef, but doesn't make meatloaf due to the whole CPR thing.

Made in United States
Troutdale, OR
12/06/2024

25949746R10120